TRANSFORMATION

TURN YOUR LIFE AROUND STARTING TODAY!

STEPHEN ARTERBURN
AND DAVID STOOP

Tyndale House Publishers, Inc.
Carol Stream, Illinois

Visit Tyndale's exciting Web site at www.tyndale.com

TYNDALE and Tyndale's quill logo are registered trademarks of Tyndale House Publishers, Inc.

Transformation: Turn Your Life Around Starting Today!

Copyright © 1998, 2006 by Stephen Arterburn and David Stoop. All rights reserved.

Cover photo copyright © by Gandee Vasan/Getty Images. All rights reserved.

Interior goldfish copyright © by Photodisc Blue/Getty Images. All rights reserved.

Stephen Arterburn photo copyright © 2001 by David Riley Associates. All rights reserved.

Designed by Joe Sapulich

Published in association with the literary agency of Alive Communications, Inc., 7680 Goddard Street, Suite 200, Colorado Springs, CO 80920.

Published in 1998 as *Seven Keys to Spiritual Renewal* by Tyndale House Publishers under ISBN 0-8423-5885-4

Transformation first published in 2006.

Unless otherwise indicated, all Scripture quotations are taken from the *Holy Bible,* New Living Translation, copyright © 1996, 2004. Used by permission of Tyndale House Publishers, Inc., Carol Stream, Illinois 60188. All rights reserved.

Scripture quotations marked NASB are taken from the *New American Standard Bible,* © 1960, 1962, 1963, 1968, 1971, 1972, 1973, 1975, 1977 by The Lockman Foundation. Used by permission.

Scripture quotations marked NIV are taken from the *Holy Bible,* New International Version®. NIV®. Copyright © 1973, 1978, 1984 by International Bible Society. Used by permission of Zondervan. All rights reserved.

Scripture quotations marked NRSV are taken from the New Revised Standard Version of the Bible, copyrighted, 1989 by the Division of Christian Education of the National Council of the Churches of Christ in the United States of America, and are used by permission. All rights reserved.

Library of Congress Cataloging-in-Publication Data

Arterburn, Stephen, date.
[Seven keys to spiritual renewal]
Transformation : turn your life around starting today! / Stephen Arterburn and David Stoop.
    p. cm.
Originally published: Seven keys to spiritual renewal. Wheaton, Ill. : Tyndale House Publishers, c1998.
ISBN-13: 978-1-4143-0776-3 (sc)
ISBN-10: 1-4143-0776-4 (sc)
1. Spiritual life—Christianity. I. Stoop, David A. II. Title.
BV4501.3.A783 2006
243—dc22   2005032028

Printed in the United States of America

12   11   10   09   08   07   06

7   6   5   4   3   2   1

Contents

INTRODUCTION

THE NEED for spiritual renewal is evident all around us. People are hungry for truth. They want to know what the spiritual life is all about. Those who have never paid much attention to spiritual things are taking note. Those who have grown complacent in their religious practices are seeking something deeper. Those who have a personal relationship with God are rekindling the fires of their devotion.

People of all ages want more out of life. They are seeking God, and they want more than a Sunday religion; they want something that will make a difference every day of their lives.

People of all faiths, or previously no faith, are looking to spiritual things. "People have a tremendous need for certainty, reassurance, and spiritual connection," says Arthur Warwick, a psychiatrist at the University of Maryland School of Medicine. Some are motivated by the hope of entering a "new age." They are easily enticed by psychic hotlines, where they hear promises of health, wealth, and happiness from impersonal voices that don't meddle in their morality. Others are driven by a sense of fear and foreboding. They are easily enticed by cults that provide security and promise transcendence but do not require (in fact do not even allow) mental involvement.

Whatever the motivation, the quest for spiritual renewal cuts across lines of gender, race, economic status, and age.

Consider what has been happening in the Christian arena: Revivals are breaking out around the globe, from the former Soviet Union to communist China. In America, "seeker-sensitive churches" welcome millions who want more out of life than consumerism offers. Promise Keepers events are drawing over a million men each year into stadiums around the country; men who once didn't get off the couch on Sunday mornings are now taking their families to church. Women of Faith, a conference that began in 1994 with a modest goal of reaching seven thousand, instead drew over thirty thousand the first year. By the third year, Women of Faith conferences, able to accommodate more than one hundred thousand women, sold out in record time. The quest for spirituality has also caused a surge in book publishing on the subject. Sales of books on spirituality and religion run second only to books on business.

Events and resources are not *creating* the desire for spiritual renewal; they are evidence that the desire exists and is pervasive.

While interest in spiritual things is up, however, there is a gap between what people are seeking and what they are experiencing. George Gallup Jr., executive director of the Princeton Religion Research Center, said his organization's surveys have identified three gaps that point to a lack of religious depth. These are the ethics gap, the knowledge gap, and the belonging gap. One reason so many people are on a spiritual quest may be their desire to fill these gaps.

Surprisingly, those who consider themselves active in religion tend *not* to live by the ethical standards of what they believe—they tend to be unaware of their faith's basic teachings; and while they profess a belief in God, they do not necessarily belong to a community of faith where they attend religious services.

Since you are reading this book, you probably don't need statistics to convince you. All the evidence you need is your own desire for spiritual renewal within your heart, mind, soul, and body. You want a deeper relationship with God, more meaningful relationships with loved ones, and the assurance that your life has value. In other words, you want faith that will transform your life.

This book presents seven keys that unlock the doors to a deeper relationship with God and thus to a renewed spiritual life that will transform your entire being and lead to the satisfaction found only in reconciliation with God. These are keys, not steps. Although we present them sequentially, they are to be used as needed. There's no reason to wait to use one—it's not as if you have to master previous ones before going on to the next one.

We did not create these concepts; they are based on principles ordained by God at Creation and revealed throughout Scripture to enable mortals to enjoy a relationship with the Immortal. Throughout the ages, the practice of these concepts has brought about spiritual renewal and transformation in countless lives. We have simply put them in a format that makes them easy to remember and easy to use.

These keys are not something you use once and discard; they are to be used daily. Whenever you encounter a situation that seems to have a lock on it, one of these keys will fit. As you become more accustomed to using them, you will more quickly recognize which one to use.

Our prayer is that with these keys you will unlock the doors blocking your access to God and keeping you from finding and fulfilling the remarkable, satisfying purpose he has in mind for you.

Chapter 1

Seek God and Surrender to Him

Our Father in heaven, may your name be kept holy.
May your Kingdom come soon.
May your will be done on earth, as it is in heaven.

Matthew 6:9-10

THE CROWDS bustled in the dusty streets, jostling him, pushing him. What was all the commotion? He pressed his portly frame through the mass of people. He was not used to being pushed around, and he didn't enjoy mingling with the masses. But he had to find out the cause of all the excitement.

Being a short man, he could not see over the heads of all the people pushing toward the street. "What is it?" he asked. "What's all the excitement about?"

A woman answered, "Jesus! Jesus of Nazareth is passing by."

Zacchaeus had heard wild stories about this Jesus, so wild in fact that he hardly could believe they were true. Now he had an opportunity to see the man for himself; he could not let it go by. So he ran ahead of the crowd and climbed up into the boughs of a sycamore-fig tree along the route Jesus would take.

What drove Zacchaeus up that tree? Curiosity? Perhaps. But it just as easily could have been spiritual hunger, the hunger known all too well by those who have learned that "having it all" isn't enough. Although Zacchaeus was rich and powerful—a chief tax collector whom the people both feared and hated—he was also needy. He needed God. He needed Jesus.

Zacchaeus was one of many who sought Jesus that day. It was a diverse assembly, but they all had one thing in common with each other and with you and me. They were seeking. Some may have been seeking a good time (word probably had spread that Jesus had turned water into wine at a wedding celebration). Some may have been seeking a handout (Jesus had made meals multiply on a Galilean hillside). Some may have been in need of physical healing (Jesus had healed a man with leprosy, the most dreaded disease of that time). Some, having reached the end of themselves, may have come needing a new start. They could have been seeking any of the many other things humans long for. The important point is, none were satisfied; they all longed to have "enough." And enough meant more—even to Zacchaeus, the one who already had more than most.

Zacchaeus probably didn't expect to be noticed by Jesus that day. More likely, he expected to be rejected by this holy man. After all, Zacchaeus was a notorious sinner. But when Jesus came by, he looked up at Zacchaeus and called him by name. "Zacchaeus!" he said. "Quick, come down! I must be a guest in your home today."

So Zacchaeus climbed down from the tree and welcomed Jesus gladly.

This caused quite a stir among the people. They were aghast that Jesus would spend time with such an evil person.

But being in the presence of Jesus caused a transformation in Zacchaeus. He stood up and said, "I will give half my wealth to the poor, Lord, and if I have cheated people on their taxes, I will give them back four times as much!"

"Salvation has come to this home today," Jesus announced, "for this man has shown himself to be a true son of Abraham. For the Son of Man came to seek and save those who are lost" (see Luke 19:1-10).

What happened to Zacchaeus is a picture of what can happen to each of us; it is indeed what needs to happen in every life—dramatic transformation and spiritual renewal.

This kind of surrender and the resulting spiritual renewal begin the same way for every person—the seemingly untroubled as well as the most desperate. It begins with hunger, with a sense that there has to be more.

Perhaps your life is completely out of control and careening toward destruction. Or perhaps you're realizing that you've been deceived by Western civilization's biggest lie: having the best of this world's "things" will bring satisfaction. Perhaps you've been treated badly by some form of organized religion and now want nothing to do with anything remotely religious. Or perhaps you go to church three times a week and still feel as if something is missing.

Soul hunger is the same whether we live in the White House or in a shelter for the homeless; whether we are the latest sex symbol or a devoted wife and mother; whether we are Bill Gates or a common working man. Whoever we are, wherever life has taken us, however much we have or don't have, we hunger for more—something richer, deeper, prettier, tastier, faster, or more satisfying.

Some people acknowledge their hunger and seek to satisfy it in socially acceptable ways: education, career, family, friends, or public service. Others, not realizing that the emptiness they feel is common to everyone, become angry and attempt to satisfy their hunger in socially unacceptable ways: illicit sex, the misuse of drugs and alcohol, or violence.

Whichever category of behavior we fall into, our need is the same: God. And the only way to have God is to surrender to him.

What Surrender Is Not

Surrender is not a bargaining tool we use to get what we want from God; surrender is giving ourselves to him. Nor is it trying to cut a deal with God: *If God will give me the "happy ending" I have scripted for my life, I will go to church and give money to charity.* That is manipulation, not surrender. Surrender is trusting God to write and direct the script of our lives.

Surrender is not conditional; it is a commitment to serve God no matter what: whether we get the job or not, whether our child dies or lives, whether we live in a rented apartment or a mansion. Surrender is choosing to be content with whatever God allows. Surrender is to God alone, not to what God can do and not to what we expect God to do.

Surrender is not impatiently waiting for God to deliver the results we demand. Instead, it is being satisfied with the results he gives; it means being content with God and the blessings of his Kingdom. God does promise to answer prayer, but if we start orchestrating our own answers when God doesn't respond in our way or in our time, we have not surrendered. Our own abilities to solve problems may lead us to believe that God will sprinkle "holy water" on our human solutions or that he will sign on as a troubleshooting consultant for our freelance problem-solving business. Not so. God calls us to surrender to him; he will not surrender to us.

Surrender is not a onetime event. "I surrender all! I surrender all! All to thee, my blessed Savior. I surrender all!" That familiar chorus represents the ideal. However, in the day-to-day reality of life, surrender needs to be an ongoing behavior; it's a process, not an event.

Those of us who have been Christians for a long time tend to think that we handled this surrender business years ago. We like to believe that surrender is for someone else, someone more desperate, someone in more trouble or more pain. Not true.

While there is a defining moment when we choose to give our lives to Christ, we must also do so continuously. The Christian life is like a marriage. On their wedding day a man and woman surrender themselves to one another. But to make the marriage work, they must yield to each other on a daily basis; they must continually remind themselves of their commitment and continuously surrender their right to have their own way.

In the Christian life daily surrender is necessary because we have a dual nature—the new nature God gives when we trust Christ as Savior, and the old, sin-inclined nature that resists submission to God's commands.

What Surrender Is

Webster's defines *surrender* in this way: "to yield to the power, control, or possession of another. . . ; to give (one-self) over to something (as an influence)."[1]

People surrender every day. They *yield* to peer pressure, and they *give themselves over* to temptation. But that kind of surrender does not open the door to spiritual renewal. The surrender we speak of involves *yielding or handing oneself up to the purposes of God and giving oneself up to the power of God's Kingdom.* Surrender is admitting that we can't handle life without God. We stop pretending to be God, get off the throne of our lives, and let God rule. In short, surrender means to obey him. We come to God on his terms, accepting that he is God and that he can do with us whatever he wants, but trusting that because he is a God of love, whatever he wants to do with us will be for our ultimate good.

Surrender means that we allow God's Holy Spirit to empower us to do the good he has planned for us to do. It is only by the power of the Holy Spirit that we can live as God intends, so surrender is a prerequisite to godly behavior. It is a process of abiding in, resting in, and yielding to Jesus—just as a branch remains connected to and abides in the vine. When we continually surrender to God in this way, our lives will bear the fruit of the Holy Spirit: love, joy, peace, patience, kindness, goodness, faithfulness, gentleness, and self-control (Galatians 5:22-23). Surrender is centering our lives on God and relying on him, not on ourselves.

Surrender is relying on others. God has made us incomplete and needing help from others, so he makes us part of a unit—the church. The biblical metaphors that illustrate this concept are numerous. We are stones in God's building, members of his family, and members of his body. All of these make the same point: We may come alone to God, but he makes us part of something much bigger than ourselves.

This idea goes against American individualism. It cuts to the heart of human pride and self-sufficiency. Some people believe they don't need anybody—including God. They chuckle when anyone suggests that they "let go and let God." The old "religion is a crutch" cliché comes easily to their lips, but only until they are bent under a burden they can no longer bear. And even when they go to him at the point of desperation, they do so only to try to get back whatever they have lost.

Surrender is impossible in a heart that is proud. Surrender requires humility, not only before God but also before fellow humans. Standing proud will keep us from bowing in surrender to the One who made us. This realization is accompanied by a powerful promise in God's Word: "Humble yourselves before the Lord, and he will lift you up in honor" (James 4:10). The principle of surrender may get more use than any other simply because it is something we need every day and in every area of life.

Conduct

A primary aspect of surrender involves personal morality. We cannot love God and at the same time replace God's code of conduct with our own preferences regarding right and wrong. Jesus said, "If you love me, you will keep my commandments" (John 14:15, NRSV). God's Word is clear: While no one perfectly obeys God's law, people who are part of his Kingdom accept his Word as the only standard for morality. To surrender, then, means to bring ourselves into agreement with God's rules and not try to adapt them to agree with our weaknesses, preferences, or political perspectives.

Some people surrender to God in their public lives but keep their private lives to themselves. For example, if an unhappily married woman spends time with attractive men other than her husband, she is leaving the door wide open to adultery, even though she hasn't explicitly said yes to the idea. In so doing, she continues her courtship with the devil, the master of seduction.

When we obey God outwardly but allow our minds and hearts to remain unsurrendered, it's only a matter of time until inward disobedience becomes outward sin.

Thoughts

God's highest commandment is to love God with heart, soul, and *mind*. This means that our thoughts are not off-limits to God's control. If we permit ongoing daydreams or infatuations to grow or if we continue to entertain fantasies of anger or vengeance, we have an area of life that needs to be surrendered.

Feelings

One of the most challenging areas of surrender is that of the emotions. People sometimes excuse themselves by saying, "I can't help it—that's just the way I felt." This kind of thinking assumes that emotions are so powerful that the will cannot stand against them. This false belief results in a lot of bad behavior, guilt, and the need for confession and restoration.

At the other extreme are those who deny their emotions. For example, Christian men who use pornography often do so as a way of having their physical needs "relieved" without risking emotional involvement with another human being. But God's design for sexual satisfaction involves two people who are bound together emotionally, mentally, spiritually, and physically. Some people pretend to everyone, including themselves, that they aren't upset, anxious, or angry, but these emotions eventually influence their actions and relationships either consciously or subconsciously.

Whether we indulge our emotions or deny them, we've got trouble. Surrender involves our whole being, and any area that is unsurrendered is a target for the enemy of the soul.

Relationships

All relationships need to be surrendered to God and be subject to his principles. Emotional involvement with certain people can create dependencies that take precedence over devotion to God or to another God-ordained relationship. If we have a relationship that we cannot pray about due to feelings of guilt, we can assume that we have *not* surrendered it to God.

Overinvolvement in a relationship may be an attempt

to play God in someone else's life. Some people think it is their role to "fix" others, either by implicit manipulation or by explicit control. They may even feel empty unless someone is dependent on them. They crave the approval—sometimes even the worship—of people in their lives, and their inability to let go reveals an unhealthy need for affection and admiration.

If we try to force relationships to happen rather than wait for God to meet our needs in his way and in his time, our clumsy attempts to please, reform, or possess people may drive them away rather than build healthy, two-way relationships.

Time

The use of time is fundamental to the surrendered life. If we speak of surrender to God on one hand while reserving our schedule, and the things we do with it, as our own, we will end up living in conflict and frustration.

Career

When commitments interfere with our ability to keep the priorities God describes in his Word, they need to be re-examined. We can even give too much of ourselves to good things like volunteerism, fitness, and church activities—perhaps to the detriment of our physical health and/or our family's well-being.

All of this boils down to one point: Surrender means that we *resign* from being the ultimate ruler of our lives and *yield* to the righteous rule of God.

Surrender to a King

Job was a "righteous man" who got caught in the middle of an argument between the Almighty and the devil. Job's blessed life was unexpectedly plagued, and he wanted to know why. What was happening didn't make sense to him. His friends all blamed him, and his wife told him to curse God and die. But Job persisted in trying to understand God. Finally—after listening to his friends give their views of God—Job heard from God himself. God didn't answer Job's questions; instead he posed some powerful questions of his own (see Job 38–40):

> Then the LORD answered Job from the whirlwind: "Who is this that questions my wisdom with such ignorant words? Brace yourself like a man, because I have some questions for you, and you must answer them. Where were you when I laid the foundations of the earth? Tell me, if you know so much. Who determined its dimensions and stretched out the surveying line? What supports its foundations, and who laid its cornerstone as the morning stars sang together and all the angels shouted for joy? Who kept the sea inside its boundaries as it burst from the womb, and as I clothed it with clouds and wrapped it in thick darkness? For I locked it behind barred gates, limiting its shores. I said, 'This far and no farther will you come. Here your proud waves must stop!' Have you ever commanded the morning to appear and caused the dawn to rise in the east? Have you made daylight spread to the ends of the earth, to bring an end to the night's wickedness?" Job 38:1-13

> Then the LORD said to Job, "Do you still want to argue with the Almighty? You are God's critic, but do you have the answers?" Then Job replied to the LORD, "I am nothing—how could I ever find the answers? I will cover my mouth with my hand. I have said too much already. I have nothing more to say." Job 40:1-5

Anyone who has a personal encounter with God has a similar response. Cornelius Plantinga Jr., dean of the Chapel of Calvin College, wrote, "The faithful evangelical preacher of God ought to say not only that God is great and

God is good, but also that God is elusive and God is strange
. . . because spiritual health depends upon it."[2]

It is dangerous to think we know God's mind, his will,
or his intentions. To fear God is, in part, to recognize his
"otherness." Yes, he revealed himself through Jesus Christ.
But he did not cease to be the mysterious and relentlessly
powerful Yahweh. It is, in fact, for this very reason that we
surrender to him. He is immeasurably greater than we are.

Surrender to a Kingdom

At one time in Israel's history the Babylonian empire sent its
army to overrun Jerusalem. God, speaking through Gedaliah,
told the people, "Do not be afraid to serve the Babylonians. . . . Settle down in the land and serve the king of Babylon, and it will go well with you" (Jeremiah 40:9, NIV).

The king of Babylon took some of the Israelites from the
royal family and the nobility to serve in his palace. They
were taught the language and literature of the Babylonians.
The king provided for them, and they were trained to enter
his service.

This was a forcible takeover, and the young men were
taken away as slaves. They surrendered without a fight
because God had said this was his will for them.

As this illustration shows, surrender means yielding to
another power. It is agreeing to serve a new king. Surrender
may involve making new friends, eating new foods, learning
a new language, obeying new rules. It encompasses the
entire being: body, mind, emotions, and will.

The surrender that leads to spiritual renewal is similar,
but with a major difference: the King to whom we yield is
entirely benevolent. When we surrender to God and yield
ourselves to his righteous rule, we place our lives under the
authority of the One who made us, loves us, and knows
what's good for us.

> Once, having been asked by the Pharisees when the kingdom of God would come, Jesus replied, "The kingdom of God does not come with your careful observation, nor will people say, 'Here it is,' or 'There it is,' because the kingdom of God is within you."
>
> Luke 17:20-21, NIV

Some people surrender to God in an attitude of defeat. Having exhausted all their own ideas and expended all their own resources, they come to God as a last resort, unable to continue the struggle on their own.

Others, like Zacchaeus and the young Israelite men, come to God at the peak of success. Yet they too must humble themselves and give themselves over as slaves of the new ruling order. They too must bow before the king.

Everyone who becomes part of God's Kingdom comes in as a slave. But here is the wondrous surprise: though we go in as slaves, God confers on us the privileges of heirs. "So you are no longer a slave, but a son; and since you are a son, God has made you also an heir" (Galatians 4:7, NIV). When we bow and acknowledge God as "Lord," as Zacchaeus did with Jesus, we receive the fullness of his Kingdom. We are his to command. And once that happens, God adopts us as his children, giving us access to the power and riches of his Kingdom.

That is why Zacchaeus suddenly became generous. Surrender made the Kingdom of God accessible to him. He was finally full, assured of having enough. Therefore, he could give freely. Spiritual renewal and transformation had taken place.

Why Avoid Surrender?

Most people fight desperately before surrendering. Some people nearly strangle themselves on the very strings they're using to pull themselves up. Why is human nature so resistant to surrender?

This is no new dilemma. The moment humans realized that self-rule was an option, surrender to God became an unpopular choice. The temptation presented to Adam and Eve is offered to each of us every day: "You will become just like God." Time and again, human beings succumb to the idea of sitting on the throne of their own lives, thinking they will be happy and fulfilled if only they can judge, control, manipulate, and operate their little corner of the universe. People in this mode of thinking have a warped view of God. They have reduced him to a genie in a bottle whose purpose is to obey their whimsical human commands. This false illusion cannot survive because all too soon the very things we seek to own or control begin destroying us. That is why this key to spiritual renewal is surrender, not control.

Every futile attempt we make to power our way through our circumstances is an act of contempt toward the One who allowed the circumstances—perhaps even designed them—to draw us into communion with himself and to develop his nature in us.

The apostle Peter explained this when he wrote,

> By his divine power, God has given us everything we need for living a godly life. We have received all of this by coming to know him, the one who called us to himself by means of his marvelous glory and excellence. And because of his glory and excellence, he has given us great and precious promises. These are the promises that enable you to share his divine nature and escape the world's corruption caused by human desires. 2 Peter 1:3-4

People want a God whose actions are predictable, a God who doesn't allow disease, bankruptcy, famines, or wars. But despite our protests, God allows these evils to exist. Surrender means accepting life as it is and submitting to God in the midst of whatever happens.

Some people fear what might happen if they surrender to God, who is unpredictable. They fear having to get along without the drug or behavior they use to ease their pain. Some fear poverty and thus grasp tightly at material things while losing their grasp on that which is eternal. Others fear obscurity or rejection or punishment. Some fear that God will not or cannot give them what they need. Some fear that God will squander their talents or keep them from reaching their goals.

John, the beloved disciple of Jesus, wrote, "There is no fear in love. But perfect love drives out fear, because fear has to do with punishment. The one who fears is not made perfect in love" (1 John 4:18, NIV).

When fear keeps us from surrendering to God, we pray that he will reveal himself as a God of love. When we see God in the light of his love, we will no longer fear surrender.

God Is Not Who We Make Him to Be

Problems with God often result from our frustration that God isn't doing things the way we want him to.

During the years when Dave and his wife struggled with one of their children, Dave kept telling God how to fix the problem, even arranging things so God could "work a miracle." When God didn't jump at the opportunity, Dave was frustrated, thinking that God wasn't who he said he was. Truthfully, Dave was frustrated because God refused to become who Dave wanted him to be. Dave eventually learned that God was much bigger than he could imagine and that God was perfectly capable of doing things his way.

God described himself to Moses as "I AM WHO I AM." The sentimentalized version of Jesus portrayed in much of the media—both religious and secular—is not a true depiction of the tough, outspoken Son of God revealed in the

Gospels. God is as he is—not as we want him to be. God, though revealed in the Bible, must also be revealed by the Holy Spirit. God cannot be fully understood or explained. He is the living God. The apostle Paul described him as "the blessed and only Ruler, the King of kings and Lord of lords, who alone is immortal and who lives in unapproachable light, whom no one has seen or can see" (1 Timothy 6:15-16, NIV).

Who Is God?

Our view of God will determine whether or not we feel safe enough to surrender to him. If we second-guess God's goodness, are unsure of his wisdom, or doubt his power, we will not release our past, present, or future into his hands. Instead, we will distance ourselves from him and continue striving on our own. But when we seek God and see him as he is, we realize that it is safe to surrender to him. So it is essential to know the true nature of God.

God is Creator

God designed us and has a unique purpose for each of our lives. David wrote of God:

> You made all the delicate, inner parts of my body and knit me together in my mother's womb. Thank you for making me so wonderfully complex! Your workmanship is marvelous—how well I know it. You watched me as I was being formed in utter seclusion, as I was woven together in the dark of the womb. You saw me before I was born. Every day of my life was recorded in your book. Every moment was laid out before a single day had passed. Psalm 139:13-16

When we realize that God has a purpose for us, we can trust that he will lead us toward that purpose when we surrender to him.

God is a refuge

Think of almighty God, whose power and presence bring terror to mere mortals, as the Creator of all that is and as Commander in Chief of all the hosts of heaven. Now think of him as being on our side (or, rather, our being on his side)! When we surrender to God, he becomes our protector—our refuge. David, king of Israel, wrote,

> Those who live in the shelter of the Most High will find rest in the shadow of the Almighty. This I declare about the LORD: He alone is my refuge, my place of safety; he is my God, and I trust him. Psalm 91:1-2

In this respect, surrender brings peace—peace preserved by God's strength.

Under our own rule, we are subject to the insecurity of self-reliance. Under God's rule, we are anchored to the One the psalmist described as "the Rock" (Psalm 89:26). That Rock is steadfast, unmovable, and worthy of all our trust.

God is love

The apostle John wrote, "Anyone who does not love does not know God, for God is love. God showed how much he loved us by sending his one and only Son into the world so that we might have eternal life through him. This is real love—not that we loved God, but that he loved us and sent his Son as a sacrifice to take away our sins" (1 John 4:8-10).

We can be sure God's plans for us are loving plans because he proved his love on the cross. There is no greater love.

God is good

God not only loves us but also works for our good when we love him in return. The apostle Paul wrote, "And we know that God causes everything to work together for the good of those who love God and are called according to his purpose for them" (Romans 8:28).

And centuries earlier the prophet Jeremiah spoke for God when he said,

> "For I know the plans I have for you," says the LORD. "They are plans for good and not for disaster, to give you a future and a hope. In those days when you pray, I will listen. If you look for me wholeheartedly, you will find me."
>
> Jeremiah 29:11-13

Since God is working out his purpose for those who love him, we can surrender to him in all circumstances—good, bad, and the seemingly impossible ones—even if we have complicated our lives with mistakes and disobedience.

God is just and merciful

Paul wrote,

> God presented Jesus as the sacrifice for sin. People are made right with God when they believe that Jesus sacrificed his life, shedding his blood. This sacrifice shows that God was being fair when he held back and did not punish those who sinned in times past, for he was looking ahead and including them in what he would do in this present time. God did this to demonstrate his righteousness, for he himself is fair and just, and he declares sinners to be right in his sight when they believe in Jesus.   Romans 3:25-26

Every human being has a sin problem that requires punishment or forgiveness. When we see God as just, we can surrender to him, confess our guilt, and know that God upholds what is right. After all, who could trust a God who winked at evil and wrongdoing? And when we see God as merciful, we need not fear surrender.

Dare We Trust Such a God?

Do we dare entrust our fragile lives to the real God of the Bible? Can we trust a God who may allow pain, does not guarantee unabated happiness, and will not tolerate any form of idolatry? If not, we will find all kinds of excuses for not surrendering to him.

Early in my life, I felt driven to use my wits to get what I wanted, which usually meant just having a good time. I created a world that looked fun and exciting but was anything but that. I was under enormous pressure to keep up the pretense. I took every talent God had given me and turned it into stress, worry, pain, and fear. The resulting guilt burdened me with doubts about my salvation and about God's love.

I had created a living hell for myself and had to fight to keep from being consumed by it. To survive, I sought new thrills and pleasures that would keep my mind sedated. Thinking was unbearable because God kept coming to mind.

All that changed in a flash when I was sitting in a seminar on conflicts within the soul. God met me there and allowed me to see the truth. I saw the consequences of my self-willed life, and I realized that I could not continue having my own way. The course I was on would lead to frustration and more destruction. But more important, I saw a way out. It was through the heart of God. I realized that God's plan for me was no easier than mine, but it offered hope rather than despair. It offered peace with God and with my own soul. To my amazement, it also offered power, the kind of power I needed to deal with the hurts and pain I had created.

So, in that moment of awareness, I surrendered my will to God. I simply said, "God, you take it. It's yours. I'm yours. Let's get on with it."

That act of surrender launched me on a journey of growth. In less than a heartbeat I was no longer trapped in a life I didn't want to live. By surrendering to God, I found a way out.

That instant of surrender was followed by growth. The growth was painful, but I knew the purpose of it was to disconnect me from my waywardness and to connect me to God and his way. More important, I found something I had not experienced since accepting Christ at age nine. I found peace. Peace engulfed me. Peace saturated my thoughts and blossomed in an irrepressible smile. What a difference!

Every tyrannical thought that had tormented me was replaced with one of grace, love, or acceptance. My role was simple: I would merely be the man God had created me to be. No, I didn't find perfection; but I found peace, and that was enough. True surrender always leads to peace.

For me, seeing my situation and my need for change coincided with seeing the heart of God.

Benefits of Surrender

When we stop trying to clean up our shattered hopes, twisted plans, and broken agendas, God has room to work. He can remove the clutter, restore the good, and bring order and beauty out of our chaos. God can be amazingly creative when we get out of his way and give him room to work.

We can be relieved of the guilt, failure, and regret that so often accompany disappointments.

When we recognize that God, and God alone, has the power to realign our lives according to his will, we will be able to relax and await his timely intervention.

Surrender to God will lead us away from sin. When we stop planting seeds of sin, we no longer will have to reap its deadly harvest. Troubles come to all, but there is devastation that strikes the ungodly with ferocity as a direct result of sin. Surrender to God will spare us this. King David wrote, "The righteous person faces many troubles, but the LORD comes to the rescue each time" (Psalm 34:19).

What Does Surrender Look Like?

When we surrender, we become like clay in God's hands. Allowing God's grace to mold us means putting our lives into his hands and saying, "Do with me as you will." This requires malleability and the willingness to accept that we may not be permitted to accomplish everything we set out to do. We may be unable to use our gifts the way we want to use them. It means allowing the potter to reshape us without our arguing. As the prophet Isaiah wrote, "Does a clay pot argue with its maker? Does the clay dispute with the one who shapes it, saying, 'Stop, you're doing it wrong!' Does the pot exclaim, 'How clumsy can you be?'" (Isaiah 45:9).

Thomas à Kempis, a fifteenth-century writer, put his life in God's hands and said:

> Do with me whatever it shall please thee. For it can not be anything but good, whatever thou shalt do with me. If it be thy will I should be in darkness, be thou blessed; and if it be thy will I should be in light, be thou again blessed. If thou grant me comfort, be thou blessed; and if thou wilt have me afflicted, be thou still equally blessed. My son such as this ought to be thy state, if thou desire to walk with Me. Thou must be as ready to suffer as to rejoice. Thou must cheerfully be as destitute and poor, as full and rich.[3]

Another picture of the surrendered life can be seen in Blaise Pascal. In 1659 Pascal began writing an apology for the Christian faith that he planned to spend the next ten years completing. A brilliant mathematician and thinker, Pascal had committed his great intelligence to pondering the mysteries of faith, the human heart, and eternity. After beginning his project, Pascal contracted a severe illness, and he was never able to develop the work as he had originally envisioned.

Rather than wrestling with God and rebelling at his unexplainable will, Pascal surrendered to the course his life had taken. He spent his last days passing out blankets and food to the poor. When he died, still a young man, he left behind his "Thoughts," the undeveloped beginning of his lifework. Today his well-known writings, entitled the *Pensées,* continue to be studied and taught by theologians and philosophers.

Though brilliant, capable, and spiritual, Pascal gave up his grand intellectual scheme and gave himself over to a life of physical service. He saw the course God had set before him and he followed it humbly, leaving the consequences with God. God did use him greatly, but not in the way he supposed. His surrender has become our example. When he humbled himself, God lifted him up to minister to the ages.

Above all other examples is Jesus himself. He surrendered to the will of his Father throughout his earthly ministry. He told his disciples, "The world must learn that I love the Father and that I do exactly what my Father has commanded me" (John 14:31, NIV). The way of surrender led him to his knees. He knew that the Cross awaited him when he knelt to pray. But listen to his prayer: "Father, if you are willing, please take this cup of suffering away from me. Yet I want your will to be done, not mine" (Luke 22:42). Then an angel appeared to him and strengthened him. But Jesus, still in anguish, prayed even more earnestly, and his sweat fell like drops of blood to the ground.

Surrender is scary *before* we do it—even when we're surrendering to Jesus—but the rewards to ourselves and to others are immeasurable. Surrender does not come without pain or struggle. But it is worth it. Hebrews 12:2-3 (NIV) says:

Let us fix our eyes on Jesus, the author and perfecter of our faith, who for the joy set before him endured the cross, scorning its shame, and sat down at the right hand of the throne of God. Consider him who endured such opposition from sinful men, so that you will not grow weary and lose heart.

A Call to Surrender

David, the mighty Hebrew king, understood that God is the supreme authority. Before God, David saw himself as a child. He wrote,

LORD, my heart is not proud; my eyes are not haughty. I don't concern myself with matters too great or too awesome for me to grasp. Instead, I have calmed and quieted myself, like a weaned child who no longer cries for its mother's milk. Yes, like a weaned child is my soul within me. Psalm 131:1-2

If mighty King David can come to God as a child, what stops us? With all our responsibilities, goals, and agendas, it may seem unrealistic. But the reality is, we don't have to imagine it; we can experience it. We can choose right now to surrender to God.

We have no reason to believe that Zacchaeus got up on that life-changing morning and said, "I think I'll surrender my life to God today. I think I'll give away my possessions and make restitution for the wrong I have done." But we do know that Zacchaeus went out of his way that day to see Jesus. And, even more surprising, Jesus went out of his way to meet Zacchaeus.

The one person who had the right to judge Zacchaeus— God incarnate—offered him forgiveness instead. And from the one person Zacchaeus expected rejection—Jesus—he received acceptance.

Zacchaeus discovered an important truth about God that

day: God was seeking him. Jesus said, "For the Son of Man came to seek and save those who are lost" (Luke 19:10).

Something took place within Zacchaeus to cause him to surrender his life and wealth to God. Something caused him to confess his sins, accept responsibility for them, and make restitution. A spark of faith ignited the truth of God's love, and his life exploded with joy and generosity. And that is just the beginning of spiritual renewal.

Notes

1. *Merriam-Webster's Collegiate Dictionary*, 10th ed. (Springfield, Mass.: Merriam-Webster, Inc., 1993), s.v. "surrender."
2. Cornelius Plantinga Jr., *Not the Way It's Supposed to Be: A Breviary of Sin* (Grand Rapids, Mich.: Eerdmans, 1995).
3. Thomas à Kempis, *The Imitation of Christ*, III:17:1-2.

START TODAY!

How to Seek God and Surrender to Him

- Humble yourself before the God of the universe
- Give up your efforts to change others and let God change you instead
- Don't insist on having your own way, but instead submit to God's way
- Admit that God is all-powerful and place your life under his control
- Admit that God is King and place your life under his righteous rule
- Submit to God's way of doing things even when you don't understand
- Seek God's Kingdom and put God first in your life
- Pray, "I want your will, not mine"
- Become childlike in your obedience to God, your heavenly Father

- Surrender your independence to join the ranks of God's people

BIBLICAL EXAMPLE
Zacchaeus

BIBLE VERSES
Matthew 6:9-10: "Our Father in heaven, may your name be kept holy. May your Kingdom come soon. May your will be done on earth, as it is in heaven."

Chapter 2
See the Truth

Search me, O God, and know my heart;
test me and know my anxious thoughts.
Point out anything in me that offends you,
and lead me along the path of everlasting life.

Psalm 139:23-24

YOUNG DAVID started out with twenty-twenty spiritual vision. God himself said of the soon-to-be king, "I have found David son of Jesse, a man after my own heart. He will do everything I want him to do" (Acts 13:22). David loved God, longed to be close to him, and willingly opened his life to God's inspection. "Search me, O God, and know my heart," he prayed. "Test me and know my anxious thoughts. Point out anything in me that offends you, and lead me along the path of everlasting life" (Psalm 139:23-24). He also said, "My steps have stayed on your path; I have not wavered from following you" (see Psalm 17:5).

But one day David's feet did slip, and he fell headlong into immorality. He saw his neighbor's wife, Bathsheba, bathing on her rooftop, and he sent for her. They had sex, and she became pregnant. David tried to cover up his sin by bringing Bathsheba's husband, Uriah, home from battle.

David was hoping that Uriah would be intimate with his wife and assume that the child she had conceived was his own. But Uriah's sense of duty to his fellow soldiers would not allow him to enjoy a privilege they did not have, so he refused to sleep with his wife. David then gave a message to the unsuspecting Uriah to take back to his commander. The message told the commander to send Uriah to the front lines of battle and then withdraw. The commander obeyed, and the noble Uriah died in battle.

David behaved as most of us do when we sin: He tried to go on with his life as if nothing had happened. He brought Bathsheba to his house, made her his wife, and awaited the birth of their child. Even with the visible evidence of his sin growing daily in his wife's womb, David did not repent. For at least nine months, God waited in vain to hear David's confession. Finally, after the child was born, God sent Nathan the prophet, David's trusted advisor, to confront the king.

Nathan used a clever technique to get David to see the seriousness of his sin. He told a story about a man who had behaved in much the same way David had.

"There were two men in a certain town," Nathan began. "One was rich, and one was poor. The rich man owned a great many sheep and cattle. The poor man owned nothing but one little lamb he had bought. He raised that little lamb, and it grew up with his children. It ate from the man's own plate and drank from his cup. He cuddled it in his arms like a baby daughter. One day a guest arrived at the home of the rich man. But instead of killing an animal from his own flock or herd, he took the poor man's lamb and killed it and prepared it for his guest."

By the time Nathan got to this point in the story, the king was enraged. "As surely as the LORD lives," he vowed, "any man who would do such a thing deserves to die! He must repay four lambs to the poor man for the one he stole and for having no pity" (see 2 Samuel 12:1-6).

David should have seen the similarity between what he had done and the story Nathan told, but he didn't. The king had what today we would call a huge blind spot. So Nathan had to make the accusation point-blank. "You are that man!" Nathan said to the king.

What happened to David shows what happens to all of us when we ignore sin. It doesn't go away; it moves in and makes itself at home. It doesn't diminish; it escalates. Some Bible commentators believe that David's sin did not begin with adultery or even with lust. They suggest that it began with something seemingly innocuous: apathy and disinterest. This idea comes from 2 Samuel 11:1: "In the spring of the year, when kings normally go out to war, David sent Joab and the Israelite army to fight the Ammonites. They destroyed the Ammonite army and laid siege to the city of Rabbah. However, David stayed behind in Jerusalem."

The key phrase here is the last one: *However, David stayed behind in Jerusalem.* Also note the apathy in verse 2: "Late one afternoon, after his midday rest, David got out of bed." If David had been where he belonged—leading his army—he would not have been taking a nap in the middle of the day or walking around on the roof of his palace where he could see his neighbor's wife taking a bath. In David's case, the seed of sin sprouted quickly and grew into a tangled mess. Once he decided to delegate authority rather than lead his army, his behavior quickly degenerated to lust, adultery, and finally murder.

As the story of David so clearly illustrates, the failure to see the truth about sin leads to ever more serious sin. The same thing happens to us when we bounce along in life and ignore the road signs that tell us we've made a wrong turn. Most of our sins are not the blatant variety; they are the subtle kind that we seldom even call sin. But left unattended, they escalate into major problems, as the following examples show.

When We Refuse to See Our Faults

For the first few years of marriage, Claire and Brent were happy. They lived in a tiny cottage with rented furniture, drove an ancient Jeep, and centered their lives on Brent and his music. Brent seldom had steady work, but he took his music seriously and practiced many hours a day.

When children came along, Claire took a full-time job so Brent could continue to pursue his dream of becoming a famous musician. Brent seldom helped with the children and worked only on occasion. Claire worked hard at the office as well as at home, and she earned numerous promotions. Over time, Brent became increasingly sarcastic and critical. Eventually he withdrew his affection from the children and lost interest in a sexual relationship with Claire.

Claire became increasingly depressed, yet she clung to Brent. Though troubled by his indifference, she yearned to see him happy and successful. Claire failed to see that the more she accomplished, the less effort Brent made. She also failed to see that her success fed Brent's irresponsibility.

For years, Claire and Brent ignored the escalating tensions between them, so the problems got worse. Claire refused to look at her own neediness and considered her tolerance of Brent a strength, not a weakness. After all, how many other women would put up with behavior like Brent's selfishness, jealousy, and lack of love for her and for their children? Claire began having serious physical problems, but doctors diagnosed her symptoms differently every time she was admitted to the hospital. Brent, still refusing to admit his own failure, was resentful when Claire's illness made it necessary for him to take a part-time job. His blind spots prevented him from seeing the reality of his situation.

When We Focus on the Faults of Others

Cheryl worked hard to maintain control of her family, especially her husband, Alex. But even when he and other family members cooperated with her, she was not happy. She still felt empty and depressed, which compelled her to be even more controlling. Cheryl was operating under the faulty assumption that she could be happy if everyone and everything around her were perfect.

Alex wanted to please Cheryl, so he often went along with her plans. But he too was unhappy and was quick to point out Cheryl's controlling personality. He had been raised by a mother who was difficult to please, and she had trained him to believe that his role was to please the primary woman in his life. Alex was operating under the faulty assumption that he would be happy if he could make either his mother or his wife happy.

While neither could see what was wrong within, both could articulate what was wrong with the other—and with anyone else who happened to come up in conversation.

Neither Alex nor Cheryl could see the true dynamics of their relationship—that each had needs the other could not be expected to meet. Cheryl needed to have someone create a perfect environment for her, and Alex needed to provide one. They were a perfect match—except for one thing: they were matched in weakness, not in strength.

Denial

Both couples were suffering from a condition called denial. Claire and Brent simply pretended that nothing was wrong, whereas Cheryl and Alex both denied any personal wrongdoing, each blaming the other for the problems in their relationship. They all ended up in despair because their blind spots kept them from seeing the truth about their problems, which also kept them from seeing any solutions.

The Complete Life Encyclopedia defines denial as "an inability to see the truth about oneself. In a sense, it is a lie people tell themselves, which, once they have told it, they cling to and believe."[1]

Denial blurs our vision of many things—troubled or destructive relationships, sins we are unwilling to acknowledge, overly optimistic goals, financial irresponsibility, physical illness, unresolved character issues, self-righteousness, and any number of other situations that we'd rather not see clearly. If we seriously desire spiritual renewal, we have to look at the entirety of life, even the areas we have closed off, and especially the lies we have convinced ourselves are true.

Denial blinds us not only to the problems we're trying to avoid but to their inevitable consequences. When we see things accurately, we also see the troubling results. This awareness often leads to depression and an overwhelming urge to find diversions and alternative ways to feel good, rather than suffer the pain of taking the necessary action.

Why We Keep Our Eyes Closed

Truth is a scary thing. Sometimes the harsh reality of it frightens us into a "see no evil" mode. For some people life has been incredibly difficult. They have survived what they hope is the worst and have no interest in further suffering. For them, denial is the only coping mechanism they know, and they would rather endure miserable circumstances than suffer the discomfort of change.

Ending denial brings with it the threat of loss as well as pain. People sometimes resist seeing the truth and accepting reality because of the high price. Accepting the consequences of truth may cause the loss of income, possessions, family, friends, or prestige. What people seldom recognize, however, is that denial has even worse consequences, such as the loss of life—emotional, spiritual, and sometimes even physical.

Pride is another factor that keeps us from seeing the truth about ourselves. "I can make it work!" is the motto of many who are losing their grip more quickly than they know. American culture has done a good job of convincing us that we are supposed to be independent and self-reliant. "I did it my way!" is a line from a song made popular by Frank Sinatra in the seventies that sums up the philosophy of many Americans. But those who claim it as their theme have an ego that overshadows truth.

Another reason people avoid self-scrutiny is because they don't want to stop doing something they know is wrong. People in this situation avoid conversations that go anywhere near the area they are trying to keep to themselves. And they certainly avoid reading the Bible and praying. They seem to believe that ignoring something is the same as being innocent of it. They also tend to use busyness as a means of denial. To avoid thinking about their lives, they keep such a hectic pace that they have no opportunity to see truth. With life whizzing by, they see very little—and feel even less. But they seldom realize the numbing effect denial is having on them.

The world offers unlimited distractions that keep us from looking at ourselves and our circumstances. Attitudes that we hide from ourselves and behaviors that we hide from others serve a purpose, but not a good one. We use them to meet a legitimate need in an unhealthy way. In other words, when we crave something that we know is not good for us, we do so because we are using it as a substitute for something we legitimately need but that is also difficult to acquire or achieve.

For example, people with an insatiable desire for clothes or possessions often have an unmet need for love but are afraid to risk involvement in relationships. Instead they invest their time and money in inanimate objects—things that cannot hurt or reject them. Other people continually demand perfection in others. Many times they are in need of forgiveness for their own imperfections.

Any intense "need" or desire for a particular activity or relationship is a sign that we should look more carefully at it. We may not know what we are using it as a substitute for, but if the thought of losing a relationship or habit makes us fearful, we ought to find out why. An important part of seeing truth is finding out what the true need is.

Claire and Brent are still together and are slowly rebuilding their marriage. Their willingness to look at their lives brought positive changes. Little by little, they are learning to open their eyes and to keep them open. Claire now sees her own neediness, insecurity, and fear. She has become aware that she married Brent because he needed her strength to compensate for his weakness. Hoping that Brent's dependence on her would keep him from leaving, she continued to nurture dependence. Meanwhile, Brent has come to see that his own insecurities were aggravated by Claire's achievements. His fears of inadequacy overwhelmed him when he was faced with the responsibilities of being a husband and father. Brent's resentment and jealousy of his wife's abilities caused him to quit trying, which made him more and more dependent. Claire and Brent were locked into a cycle of destruction that was pulling them downward with ever-increasing speed.

The outcome for Cheryl and Alex was quite different. Alex sought help to find a better way to live. Relieved of the need to create a perfect world for Cheryl, he found a new freedom. Sadly, when Cheryl could no longer control Alex, she left. She is still searching for someone to make life perfect for her.

Seeing the Truth about Ourselves

When the light of God's truth shines on human weakness and failure, we see the futility of self-righteousness and realize that the only sensible response is to stop pretending things aren't so bad. They are! Spiritual renewal and transformation require that we repent, which means to acknowledge and turn from our sins. But we cannot truly repent until we see ourselves as we are—as we *all* are—flawed, unholy, in need of redemption and complete reformation.

It is, after all, our shortcomings, losses, failures, fears, and needs that drive us to God. Rarely do people seek God when life is problem free. Seldom do they appreciate his love when they are surrounded by friends and family. Rarely do they appreciate his grace and forgiveness when they are not suffering the consequences of their sin.

Many people who get started in the process of renewal get stuck because they are unwilling to make an assessment of themselves; for people who believe in nothing beyond themselves, the idea of conducting a searching moral inventory is a frightening thing. Here is the apostle Paul's description of what they will find:

> Their lives became full of every kind of wickedness, sin, greed, hate, envy, murder, quarreling, deception, malicious behavior, and gossip. They are backstabbers, haters of God, insolent, proud, and boastful. They invent new ways of sinning, and they disobey their parents. They refuse to understand, break their promises, are heartless, and have no mercy. They know God's justice requires that those who do these things deserve to die, yet they do them anyway. Worse yet, they encourage others to do them, too.
>
> Romans 1:29-32

We like to think that those words are describing people who resist the truth about God—not God-fearing people like ourselves. But keep reading. Paul closes his argument with a statement that includes everyone:

> As the Scriptures say, "No one is righteous—not even one. No one is truly wise; no one is seeking God. All have turned away; all have become useless. No one does good, not a single one." Romans 3:10-12

Paul's goal in this passage is to make sure that all of us see our desperate need for God and for the salvation and forgiveness only he can offer. If we think we are a cut above the rest, we remain deluded, as did the man in this story:

> An elderly man who was very nearsighted thought of himself as an expert in evaluating art. One day he visited a museum with some friends. He had forgotten his glasses and couldn't see the pictures clearly, but that didn't stop him from airing his strong opinions. As soon as they walked into the gallery, he began critiquing the various paintings.
>
> Stopping before what he thought was a full-length portrait, he began to criticize it. With an air of superiority he began, "The frame is altogether out of keeping with the picture. The man is too homely and shabbily dressed. In fact, it was a great mistake for the artist to select such a shoddy subject for his portrait."
>
> The old fellow was babbling on and on when his wife finally managed to get to him and pull him aside. She whispered to him, "My dear, you are looking in a mirror."[2]

The Bible calls itself a mirror; it shows us what kind of people we are. We all like to think of ourselves as having only minor flaws. But that is untrue, and we can't begin the process of renewal until we see ourselves honestly. God's light illuminates our imperfections, and it is these imperfections—often the seemingly minor ones—that are the source of our greatest sin.

Getting to the truth in a previously unexamined life will take us through the hurt of loss, abuse, shame, or disappointment. But spiritual healing cannot begin without an accurate diagnosis, which comes by looking to God in order to see ourselves.

> O LORD, you have examined my heart and know everything about me. You know when I sit down or stand up. You know my thoughts even when I'm far away. . . . You know what I am going to say even before I say it, LORD.   Psalm 139:1-4

Seeing truth and accepting reality will cause discomfort, not giddy excitement or a surge of ambition. But spiritual renewal results when our discomfort leads us to the Cross and, ultimately, to the crucifixion of self, as the apostle Paul described when writing to the church in Galatia: "My old self has been crucified with Christ. It is no longer I who live, but Christ lives in me. So I live in this earthly body by trusting in the Son of God, who loved me and gave himself for me" (Galatians 2:20).

Daily death to self is the beginning of life filled with the power of the living Christ.

Seeing the truth about our own condition is one side of this key to spiritual renewal. But if we see only the truth about ourselves, we're left in a hopeless situation. Seeing the truth about God's provision is the other side.

Seeing the Truth about God

Saul of Tarsus thought he knew all about God. As a Pharisee, he was a respected religious leader who kept the law so well that no one could point out a single fault in him. But a startling encounter with the living God brought Saul into

35

the brilliant light of truth that showed him how wrong he had been.

When the new sect of Judaism sprang up—the one claiming that Jesus of Nazareth, the one crucified for the sin of blasphemy, was the long-awaited Messiah—Saul took it upon himself to rid the world of this teaching, which he considered false and dangerous. Saul was zealous against the followers of Jesus and even participated in the stoning death of one of them, a young man named Stephen. When the burgeoning faith began to spread beyond Jerusalem, Saul headed for Damascus, Syria, to get permission to arrest the followers of Jesus and take them to Jerusalem for trial.

On the road to Damascus, Saul was blinded by a flash of light. He fell to the ground and heard a voice from heaven ask, "Saul! Saul! Why are you persecuting me?"

"Who are you, lord?" Saul asked.

And the voice replied, "I am Jesus, the one you are persecuting! Now get up and go into the city, and you will be told what you must do" (Acts 9:4-6).

Saul stumbled to his feet. For the next three days he remained physically blind, but for the first time he was beginning to see spiritually. The things he had considered false he now saw to be true. And in light of that truth, Saul had to reexamine everything else he believed.

Before seeing Jesus, Saul considered himself nearly faultless. In reference to his early life, he wrote,

> If others have reason for confidence in their own efforts, I have even more! I was circumcised when I was eight days old. I am a pure-blooded citizen of Israel and a member of the tribe of Benjamin—a real Hebrew if there ever was one! I was a member of the Pharisees, who demand the strictest obedience to the Jewish law. I was so zealous that I harshly persecuted the church. And as for righteousness, I obeyed the law without fault. Philippians 3:4-6

Prior to his encounter with the living God, Saul believed that God demanded perfect obedience to the law. Therefore, he dared not admit any sinfulness, and he avoided behavior that blatantly violated the law. However, because Saul was as imperfect as the next guy, he couldn't avoid sin altogether. Ironically, his avoidance of sin became the source of his sins—pride and self-righteousness. But after Saul saw the truth and accepted the reality that Jesus Christ was the risen Son of God, everything changed! He experienced a remarkable spiritual transformation, and he became a saint, a missionary, an apostle, and an inspired writer of Scripture.

So dazzling was the glory of Jesus Christ revealed to Saul, so humbling was the truth God revealed to him about his own character, that Saul saw his own unrighteousness themoment he saw the righteousness of God. As a result, Saul's life changed so dramatically that God even changed his name. Saul became the apostle Paul. Saul, the proud man who admitted no weakness, became Paul, the humble man who bragged about it: "I am glad to boast about my weaknesses, so that the power of Christ can work through me. That's why I take pleasure in my weaknesses, and in the insults, hardships, persecutions, and troubles that I suffer for Christ. For when I am weak, then I am strong" (2 Corinthians 12:9-10).

Having seen the reality of God's provision, Paul chose to be honest about his own imperfect condition:

> I have discovered this principle of life—that when I want to do what is right, I inevitably do what is wrong. I love God's law with all my heart. But there is another power within me that is at war with my mind. This power makes me a slave to the sin that is still within me. Oh, what a miserable person I am! Who will free me from this life that is dominated by sin and death? Thank God! The answer is in Jesus Christ our Lord. . . . So now there is no condemnation for those

who belong to Christ Jesus. And because you belong to him, the power of the life-giving Spirit has freed you from the power of sin that leads to death.   Romans 7:21–8:2

Once Paul saw the truth of God's power, he dared to see the truth of his own weakness. Once he saw that God's grace was sufficient, he dared to accept his own insufficiency. All of us must do the same.

The light that blinded Saul on that dusty journey to Damascus was the light that illuminated his path forever afterward.

Living in Light and Truth

Throughout Scripture, truth and light are inextricably linked. For example, "God is light, and there is no darkness in him at all. So we are lying if we say we have fellowship with God but go on living in spiritual darkness; we are not practicing the truth" (1 John 1:5-6).

To live truthfully we must walk in the light of God's wisdom, which God promises to all who ask without doubting. Wisdom may come through prayer, reflection, and daily observance, or it may come through those who are kind enough to speak the truth in love.

Jesus promised, "When the Spirit of truth comes, he will guide you into all truth" (John 16:13). No person can discern truth rightly apart from the revelation of the Holy Spirit. Saul of Tarsus thought he knew truth, but it was not until God revealed it that he could see it.

In preparation to receive truth, we need to ask God for the following:

Humility

We must first be prepared to see our own weakness and sinfulness and not insist on our own rightness in a situation.

God is just as displeased by our stubborn refusal to examine ourselves and admit wrongdoing as he is with blatant sins. Jesus' most acrimonious words were directed to the proud Pharisees who refused to see their pride, not to the humble prostitutes and publicans who knew all too well the flaws in their character.

A teachable heart

Whenever we think we know it all, we can safely assume that we're wrong. In fact, Paul advises anyone who claims to have worldly wisdom to become a fool instead. The reason he gives is this: "For the wisdom of this world is foolishness to God" (1 Corinthians 3:19).

Someone to help you see truth

People who are truly good friends will tell us the truth if we have the courage to ask them. But we must be sure we are truly willing to hear it before we ask. If our friends are afraid to tell us, a support group or a counselor may provide the necessary honesty. All of us need someone in our lives who can tell us the unpleasant truth about ourselves without fear of losing our friendship or damaging the relationship.

Spiritual Blindness

The Bible has numerous accounts of blind people who received sight when they encountered Jesus or his disciples. One of them, Bartimaeus, is a good metaphor for spiritual blindness.

When Jesus and his disciples were leaving Jericho, blind Bartimaeus was sitting by the roadside begging. When he found out that Jesus was coming by, he began to shout, "Jesus, Son of David, have mercy on me!"

Many told him to be quiet, but he shouted all the more, "Son of David, have mercy on me!"

Jesus noticed the man and said, "Come here."

The blind man jumped to his feet and moved toward Jesus.

"What do you want me to do for you?" Jesus asked.

"Teacher, I want to see," Bartimaeus answered.

"Go," said Jesus, "your faith has healed you."

Immediately Bartimaeus received his sight and followed Jesus along the road. (Adapted from Mark 10:46-52.)

This story suggests five things we can do if we are spiritually blind:

- Call out to Jesus.
- Move as close to him as we can.
- Tell him that we want to see.
- Trust him to answer the request.
- Keep following Jesus.

Words from the prophet Isaiah assure us that God longs to lead us out of blindness:

> I will lead blind Israel down a new path, guiding them along an unfamiliar way. I will brighten the darkness before them and smooth out the road ahead of them. Yes, I will indeed do these things; I will not forsake them. Isaiah 42:16

God knows we are likely to stumble until our vision is fully restored, so he accompanies us on our journey and smooths out the rough places. He dispels our inner darkness with his Word and illuminates each step of the way.

Opening our eyes to see the truth about ourselves is a key to spiritual renewal. Seeing the truth about God and accepting his provision for sin are turning the key in the lock. And the promise that is released comes directly from Jesus, who said, "The truth will set you free" (John 8:32).

This kind of freedom is what spiritual renewal is all about. That's the truth King David discovered.

Notes

1. Stephen Arterburn, Paul Meier, and Frank Minirth, *The Complete Life Encyclopedia* (Nashville, Tenn.: Nelson, 1995).
2. M. R. De Haan, M.D., "The Mirror," *Our Daily Bread*, 24 April 1997.

START TODAY!

How to See the Truth
- Ask God to give you eyes to see the truth as he sees it
- Become willing to look at the problems in your life
- Realize that what you criticize in others is a clue to your own blind spots
- Look at what you have done in light of God's mercy and grace
- See clearly what you once were
- See clearly what you are in Christ
- See the truth about your sinful human condition
- See the truth about God's provision for your condition

BIBLICAL EXAMPLE
David's encounter with the prophet Nathan

BIBLE VERSES
Psalm 139:23-24: "Search me, O God, and know my heart; test me and know my anxious thoughts. Point out anything in me that offends you, and lead me along the path of everlasting life."

Chapter 3

Speak the Truth

Confess your sins to each other and pray for each other
so that you may be healed.

James 5:16

KING DAVID'S impulsive action had a high price tag. One
man paid for it with his life, and David paid for it with his
health and self-respect. He tried to make the best of it; he
patched it up as best he could by marrying the woman he'd
gotten pregnant and giving her and the baby a home in his
palace. But still something was wrong. David described himself as being weak, miserable, and exhausted. His "strength
evaporated like water in the summer heat" (Psalm 32:4).

Whether David didn't know what was wrong or
whether he was too stubborn to admit it, we don't know.
We do know, however, that God intervened by sending the
prophet Nathan to show David what an evil thing he had
done.

As soon as Nathan pointed it out to him, David saw the
truth. But what would he do with it? He could continue the
sin by calling Nathan a liar and denying it, or he could
bring the sin to a screeching halt by admitting it.

Unlike most people who are confronted so boldly with their sinfulness, David was quick to acknowledge his guilt. He did not rationalize his behavior, minimize its seriousness, harden his heart, or blame anything or anyone but himself. When confronted with the reality of his sin, David humbly said, "I have sinned against the LORD" (2 Samuel 12:13). At the moment David saw the seriousness of his sin, he also saw his need for God's mercy and forgiveness, and he expressed it eloquently in this psalm:

Have mercy on me, O God,
    because of your unfailing love.
Because of your great compassion,
    blot out the stain of my sins.
Wash me clean from my guilt.
    Purify me from my sin.
For I recognize my rebellion;
    it haunts me day and night.
Against you, and you alone, have I sinned;
    I have done what is evil in your sight.
You will be proved right in what you say,
    and your judgment against me is just.
For I was born a sinner—
    yes, from the moment my mother conceived me.
But you desire honesty from the womb,
    teaching me wisdom even there.

Purify me from my sins, and I will be clean;
    wash me, and I will be whiter than snow.
Oh, give me back my joy again;
    you have broken me—
    now let me rejoice.
Don't keep looking at my sins.
    Remove the stain of my guilt.
Create in me a clean heart, O God.
    Renew a loyal spirit within me.
Do not banish me from your presence,
    and don't take your Holy Spirit from me.

> Restore to me the joy of your salvation,
>   and make me willing to obey you.
> Then I will teach your ways to rebels,
>   and they will return to you.
>
> Psalm 51:1-13

The word *confess* carries with it the idea of being "found out," and people would rather let portions of their lives mildew and decay than open a window to the light of the outside world and risk having others see their dark side. But the very thing that frightens people—the light—is the thing that can heal them. By breaking silence and speaking the truth about ourselves to another person, we move out of darkness into light.

Secrecy, when applied to our sin, brings sickness into our life. Confession is God's way of healing it. God desires openness and vulnerability among his people because he wants them healthy. That's why healing is impossible until we are willing to confess.

In 1551, the Council of Trent declared:

> When Christ's faithful strive to confess all the sins that they can remember, they undoubtedly place all of them before the divine mercy for pardon. But those who fail to do so and knowingly withhold some, place nothing before the divine goodness for remission: "for if the sick person is too ashamed to show his wound to the doctor, the medicine cannot heal what it does not know."

Secrets are the last domain of a person's control. People who are quick to divulge other people's secrets vow to go to the grave with their own. But keeping secrets keeps us isolated—from God and from others. However, one simple act of vulnerability can change everything. It begins with a statement like one of these: "There's something I've never told you or anyone else." Or, "I need to tell you something that is very hard for me to say." These simple expressions can begin a spiritual transformation.

Brad and Carol had been married for less than a year when Brad started feeling uncomfortable being close to Carol. The more emotional intimacy she wanted from him, the more uncomfortable he felt. He worked, played golf, surfed the Internet, talked on the phone, and withdrew into himself—anything but relate to his wife.

He could hardly admit it to himself, but he had grown to despise Carol. The things that once attracted him to her now irritated him: the way she clung to him, hovered over him, and tried to get into anything and everything he did. She was making him feel exactly the way his mother had.

Brad's father had worked many hours and was often away from home. As a result, his mother came to rely on her children for emotional support. In horror, Brad realized that he had become a lead character in act two of the drama he'd watched as a child. Feeling trapped in a role he did not want to play, he hid the sorry situation from everyone.

Then he began attending a men's prayer group. At the third meeting, some of the men began telling about their personal struggles. One of them was involved in a lengthy battle with his daughter regarding her drug problems. Another confessed to having had a sexual liaison with a coworker. Listening to the others made Brad long to expose his own struggle. But he waited two more weeks—until a kind, older man asked, "And how can we pray for you, Brad?" Then the story poured out.

Instead of feeling humiliated, Brad felt relieved. The men were surprisingly supportive. In fact, two told him afterward that they had faced similar problems. One had resolved it; the other was still trying.

In the weeks and months to come, Brad developed the habit of telling the men at the prayer group about the developments in his marriage, both good and bad. Sometimes the men brought him to task for detrimental things in his behavior that he could not see. Other times they comforted, prayed for, and encouraged him.

His prayer group saw him through his painful ordeal, assuring him that God had the power to restore relationships, no matter how difficult the circumstances might be. Slowly Brad learned to separate Carol's legitimate needs for intimacy from his mother's unhealthy dependencies. Then, to his amazement, he fell in love with Carol all over again. Three years later Brad and Carol renewed their vows in front of the congregation, including the men's prayer group.

Brad's life began to change when he opened his heart to his prayer partners and told the truth about his struggle. "It wasn't easy," he says, "but it was the smartest thing I ever did. Confession *is* good for the soul."

What Is Confession?

The New Testament Greek word translated "confess" is *homologeo*, which means "to speak the same thing" (*homos*, same; *lego*, to speak).[1]

To say the same thing God says means to agree with him about what he says is right and wrong. When we confess sin, therefore, we are agreeing with God as to what is wrong with us. When we agree with God about this, we can personalize our confession and acknowledge the areas of our life that are not in agreement with him.

Confession has two aspects: speaking the truth about ourselves and speaking the truth about God. When speaking the truth about ourselves results in discouragement because we've had to admit failure, we can encourage ourselves by confessing the corresponding truth about God that addresses our failure. For example, if we are confessing the sin of greed, we can also confess God's promise: "This same God who takes care of me will supply all your needs from his glorious riches, which have been given to us in Christ Jesus" (Philippians 4:19).

Confession also has two audiences: God and fellow believers.

Confessing to God

God has a purpose for confession. By confessing our sin, we align ourselves with him. To be useful participants in God's work, we must agree with what he's doing in the world and how he's doing it. If we are unwilling to follow his game plan, we can't claim to be on his team.

God requires confession as a condition for salvation

No one can receive God's forgiveness without agreeing with him about two things: our own sinfulness and God's righteousness.

> If we confess our sins to him, he is faithful and just to forgive us our sins and to cleanse us from all wickedness.
>
> 1 John 1:9

> If you confess with your mouth that Jesus is Lord and believe in your heart that God raised him from the dead, you will be saved. For it is by believing in your heart that you are made right with God, and it is by confessing with your mouth that you are saved.   Romans 10:9-10

God allows us to choose whose righteousness we will be judged by—our own or Christ's. Those of us who cling to our own righteousness will fall far short of what we need to make ourselves acceptable to God, but those of us who confess our unrighteousness and cling instead to Christ's righteousness will be welcomed into God's presence.

God requires confession as a means to intimacy

No one can get close to another human being while withholding secrets from that person. In the same manner, no one can get close to God while withholding anything from him. When we give up everything *we are* to make room for everything *he is,* we gain intimacy with him because we become one with him. In other words, we come into agreement with him.

In one sense, confession does not benefit God; he already knows our thoughts so he doesn't learn anything from hearing us admit them. But it benefits him indirectly because it benefits us—his body, the church. Confession increases our honesty, heightens our understanding of the seriousness of sin, makes us more understanding of others, enables others to keep us accountable, and builds unity in the church.

Confessing to Others

Sometimes people convince themselves that confession to another human being is unnecessary. They've admitted their sin to God and they assume that's good enough. This kind of thinking ignores the clear direction James gave us: "Confess your sins to each other and pray for each other so that you may be healed. The earnest prayer of a righteous person has great power and produces wonderful results" (James 5:16).

The act of speaking the truth to each other—identifying beliefs, finding words to describe them, and entrusting those words to another person—generates accountability and unity. It brings other people into our lives and enables the body of Christ to act as a single unit. Verbal confession to another human being has benefits we cannot gain in any other way.

Confession makes sin more real to us

Putting our story into words has inherent value because when we speak, we also hear. This makes what happened more real because in listening to ourselves we involve another one of our senses. The sin is no longer a secret, a memory, an emotion, or a thought; it has existence in the physical realm. At times we might say, "I can't find the words." But as we struggle to put feelings into words, those feelings become less mysterious, less slippery, and more manageable.

Confession helps people know how to pray for us

As James wrote, healing comes as a result of prayer (5:16). God wants his people to pray for one another. But to pray effectively, people must know our spiritual and emotional needs as well as our physical needs.

Confession helps people know how to encourage us

God wants us to receive the encouragement that other people provide. Loving friends can extend words of hope, faith, confidence, and grace—the kind of messages that we cannot send to ourselves. Others can see good in us that we are too close to see in ourselves.

Confession helps people know how to counsel us

Another Christian may know biblical principles that can be translated into solutions to our problems. "There is safety in having many advisers" (Proverbs 11:14). We are not obligated to take the advice of every person who offers it, but we can gain insight from the advice, encouragement, and even the struggles of others.

Fears That Block Confession

Some people grew up in families that kept secrets about alcohol or substance abuse, immorality, violence, or financial woes. They were taught by example to be secretive. Some were even told to lie about family secrets and were threatened with harm if a secret ever got out. They learned that it was safer to remain distant from people than to risk the consequences of "spilling" the secret. As a result, some became withdrawn and others became superficial.

Whenever our emotions are disrespected, mocked, or disputed, we learn to hide them. And we usually continue to do so even if we eventually find a safe environment. Lessons learned in childhood—good or bad—are difficult to unlearn.

There are many seemingly good reasons for remaining silent instead of confessing. But when we look at them honestly, we see that they are based on fear, not faith.

Fear of losing our reputation

The fear of being publicly exposed can keep us awake at night with feelings of dread. Revealing failures to even one person and admitting that we have fallen short of perfection might result in rejection. This is a valid reason for fear, but it is not a valid reason to avoid confession. It is still better to be "found out," even to have a damaged reputation, than to allow venomous secrets to poison our relationships with God and others. We can counteract this fear by getting to know God better. When we are convinced that God is who he says he is—forgiving, protecting, able to deliver, and eager to restore—fear will diminish because we will trust him to respond according to his character.

Fear of losing our favorite sin

Another reason we recoil from confession is that it requires us to renounce unhealthy habits. Sin is incompatible with spiritual renewal, and those of us who seek God must leave behind everything that detracts from or works against God's purpose for our lives. Habits and relationships that do not enhance our spirituality detract from it. When we confess sinful attitudes, behaviors, or relationships, we must also take steps to abandon them.

Fear of losing our security

When our emotional or financial security is linked to something sinful, naturally we will fear confession. Confession will bring change, and the immediate change may not seem good. This is where faith comes in. If we agree with God about what he says is good, we can trust that the ultimate outcome of obedience will be good as well. Change brings new beginnings, new opportunities, new insights. Without change, things may not get worse, but they'll definitely not get better; stagnation is the best we can hope for.

Keeping sin secret has damaging consequences. When King David was keeping secret his sin with Bathsheba, it affected him physically. Here's how he described it: "When I refused to confess my sin, my body wasted away, and I groaned all day long. Day and night your hand of discipline was heavy on me. My strength evaporated like water in the summer heat" (Psalm 32:3-4).

Even David didn't confess until he had to. Only after the prophet Nathan confronted him did he speak the essential words, "I have sinned against the LORD" (2 Samuel 12:13).

David later wrote the rest of the poem that so eloquently expresses the beauty of confession: "Finally, I confessed all my sins to you and stopped trying to hide my guilt. I said to myself, 'I will confess my rebellion to the LORD.' And you forgave me! All my guilt is gone" (Psalm 32:5).

Many times, confrontation precedes confession. When

a family member, spouse, prayer partner, or friend points out something wrong in our lives, we have two choices: deny it or admit it. To deny it will only delay the process and make the inevitable consequences worse. To admit it will start the healing process.

An even better choice, however, is to confess and renounce sin before being confronted. Doing so will spare us considerable pain, shame, and embarrassment.

Finding a Trustworthy Confidant

Having now expounded on the importance of confession, I want to be quick to add that this is not an all-encompassing command. I am not advocating that you confess everything to everyone. Confession is not "spilling your guts" to anyone nosy enough to listen. In fact, you should never confess to anyone who is not spiritually mature.

Confession is an act of trust. We are placing our spiritual well-being into the care of another person. This makes us highly vulnerable. Therefore, the person to whom we confess must be able to keep our confession confidential. If we cannot trust our confidant, we will not risk full disclosure. And to be of value, confession must be complete.

Spiritual maturity is indicated by a number of attributes. Look for the following when seeking a confidant:

Humility

Look for someone who does not try to impress people. A person who is trying to make others think he or she is important may be tempted to divulge your personal information to gain prestige. Proud, self-righteous people are more concerned about themselves and their image than about your needs and struggles. They may even use your confession against you if it serves them well. People who make a show of their faith do not make the best confidants.

Optimism

A good confidant will have a positive attitude toward life. A negative, fearful, or unhappy person will shadow all conversations with pessimism and woe. This kind of attitude can erode faith that is already fragile. Optimism is evidence of godliness because it indicates belief in God's overriding goodness and grace.

Concern

If someone competes with you or has talked badly about you, avoid making that person your confidant. He or she will have little interest in really helping you. Find someone who has genuine concern for you but who won't allow that concern to keep him or her from being honest with you.

Honesty

Stay away from anyone who might have a hidden agenda. If someone has something to gain by befriending you, keep looking. Do not confess to anyone who could use the information to his or her own advantage. Doing so would be to place unnecessary temptation in the person's path.

Along the same line, examine your own motives regarding the person you ask to be your confidant. For example, if your bad choices have placed you on the verge of bankruptcy, a sudden urge to tell your troubles to the wealthiest person in the church probably indicates a hidden agenda—and not a very well hidden one at that.

Strength

It will be tempting to choose a weak person as a confidant because then you won't feel so bad about yourself. Avoid anyone whom you can manipulate into feeling sorry for you. Others who are needy and emotionally unstable may latch on to you to fill some unmet need in their lives. You may be more emotionally needy than you realize, so beware of becoming overly reliant on any one person. Also beware of people who appear strong but are really just controlling. Their willingness to help may turn out to be an offer to run your life.

Ultimately, it is God who delivers us from our difficulties. Although he uses other people, it is God who deserves our ultimate trust.

Availability

The person in whom you confide should not be so busy that he or she cannot be reached. The person also should live near you (at least in the same city), and your lives should intersect at some point (church, work, school, neighborhood). Proximity will give the person an opportunity to observe your behavior and confront you about anything that seems suspicious.

At the other end of the availability spectrum are people of the opposite sex. Consider them unavailable as confidants. Unhealthy infatuations and emotional attachments are likely to develop when you make yourself vulnerable to someone of the opposite sex. You can avoid these dangerous entanglements by confiding in someone of the same gender.

Many male pastors avoid counseling women due to the great potential for trouble. Besides, in most cases, women are better able to understand women and men to understand men, and that understanding is of immense value when problems need to be solved.

Spirituality

Before you seek solace, encouragement, or spiritual direction from anyone, make sure the person believes the way you do. If you fail to do this, you will be adding more confusion to your life than you are eliminating. If you are unsure what you believe, look for someone whose beliefs are consistent with his or her behavior and whom others respect.

This is a rather long list of qualifications for a confidant. If you are unable to identify someone who meets these criteria, you may want to enlist the help of a Christian counselor. This is particularly true if you are dealing with complex issues. The guarantee of confidentiality is an added benefit of professional counsel. One caution however: Make sure the counselor is committed to the truth of God's Word.

Principles for Healthy Confession

When Linda was in her late forties, she left her husband after years of frustration and arguing. For a while she tried to hide the truth from her friends, but after a particularly terrible day she confided in Cindy, a friend with whom she was having coffee.

"I'm so glad to get this off my chest," Linda admitted, drying her eyes. "It's so hard to be alone. Not having anyone to talk to is almost worse than all the fighting Ken and I did."

"You need to talk," Cindy assured Linda. "Call me whenever you need to. I want to be here for you."

Linda took Cindy up on her offer—and then some. She called Cindy morning, noon, and night. On at least two occasions, she phoned after midnight. To make matters worse, she told details about Ken that were more intimate than Cindy needed to know. Linda expected Cindy to advise her about every aspect of the situation. At times she seemed to expect Cindy to know what Ken was thinking.

After two months of this, Cindy had had enough. And her husband had had more than enough. "Lose her!" he shouted after the phone interrupted dinner for the tenth consecutive night. "Unload that woman! She's driving us all nuts!"

To handle the situation, Cindy started letting Linda's calls go directly to voice mail and stopped calling her back. Linda, of course, was devastated. Cindy, though relieved to be rid of Linda, felt guilty for how she had treated her.

The situation wound up in a mess for two reasons: Linda didn't know how to engage a confidant, and Cindy didn't know how to be one. As a result, Linda's bad situation became even worse, and Cindy's kind offer to help blew up in her face.

Linda violated three of the six principles that ought to be observed by every person who chooses to confide in another.

Be sensitive

Don't overburden your listener. People who are suffering are self-absorbed; their pain keeps their attention focused on themselves, their problems, and their needs. In fact, they have difficulty thinking about anything else. But pain is not a license to inflict discomfort on anyone else—especially someone who wants to help. Those who agree to help have lives of their own, and we are not entitled to dump our troubles on them every time we feel the need.

When you begin to confide in another person, ask how you can respect his or her time. Find out when to call and when not to. Learn the person's schedule so you can avoid asking for time or favors that will be disruptive. Agree in advance that if you call at an inopportune moment, you will not have hurt feelings when the person tells you he or she can't talk right then.

Be discreet

Use care in deciding what is appropriate to talk about and what is not. Avoid explicit sexual details, endless recitals of someone else's faults, and repetition of the same frustrating events. These are unnecessary for your listener to hear. Become a self-censor so that you don't become unwelcome.

Be honest

Don't confess someone else's sin. What Linda really needed to confess were the things she had done that contributed to the breakup of her marriage. Instead, her focus remained on the actions of her husband. This tactic allowed her to play the innocent victim who didn't need to change. If you insist on being a victim, your confession will always be shallow, and your spiritual progress will be slow at best.

Set reasonable expectations

Don't expect more than the listener is able to give. If your listener is not a trained counselor, he or she cannot be your therapist. And even a therapist is not a miracle worker. Your expectations from those who listen to your troubles should be limited and realistic, which means that you see them as listeners, not fixers. Listeners who take on the responsibility of solving another person's problems become emotionally drained.

Don't stifle your emotions

Some men and women have difficulty expressing their feelings. They may be afraid that if they begin to talk about their feelings, they will be overwhelmed by the pain. So they work hard to keep the feelings away. The best way to do this, of course, is to not talk about the pain. But that will not make it go away. Never withhold your emotions just because you don't feel like expressing them.

If you do not confess the emotions associated with truth, you fail to speak the whole truth. Feelings are a large part of your story. It is deceptive to deny your emotions, refuse to weep, hide your anger, smile over your sadness, or bluster through real fears. Besides, these are counterproductive to expressing the truth. Tears and rage are not signs of weakness or of being unspiritual. They are authentic human responses to pain and shame. Never let the desire to appear strong keep you from being honest.

Maintain healthy independence

Both Cindy and Linda got caught in an unhealthy dependency. Anyone who behaves like Linda—feeling driven to keep calling, asking for advice, reaching out for positive strokes—is placing her dependency on others, not on God. And anyone who behaves like Cindy—allowing someone else to dominate her time—shows signs of allowing her own needs and unresolved issues to get in the way of being a good listener.

Another kind of dependency can develop if the person you are talking to begins to use you and your problems as entertainment (as in a real-life soap opera), as a cause, or as a distraction from his or her own life.

Some people are born rescuers. But if they rescue out of a need to be in control or to feel important, you are likely to become too important to them. If you see that someone is becoming too attached to you, distance yourself so that the relationship can remain positive and mutually rewarding.

It All Began with Telling the Truth

Peter started using drugs when he was still in middle school, and his recreational use quickly developed into a habit. His loving Christian parents were so removed from the drug culture that they failed to recognize the warning signs until the problem was advanced.

One day Peter's mother discovered hypodermic needles in his room. Further investigation revealed other drug paraphernalia. Peter's heartsick parents confronted him with the evidence, but for several days he angrily denied everything. Then one Saturday morning Peter got out of bed early, stumbled into the kitchen, and said to his mother, "I need to talk to you and Dad."

Peter confessed to his parents that he was using several different drugs. He didn't think he could stop without help, and he was afraid to try. He didn't want to go through withdrawal, and he didn't want to lose his friends.

His parents didn't know much about drugs, but they knew enough to get Peter into a rehabilitation center the same day. Their son's healing didn't happen immediately. There were angry therapy sessions and raging scenes at home. Peter had two major relapses. At times the fear and despair almost pulled all of them under. But finally, after becoming a Christian, Peter found freedom. He has remained drug-free for several years.

Without hesitation, Peter now says, "Once I heard myself telling my parents that I was a druggie, I was on my way out of it. Just saying the words made the situation real to me. And once I faced the reality, I was ready to do whatever it took to get over it."

Before speaking the truth, Peter tried to maintain independence and secrecy. In contrast, *by* speaking the truth, Peter acknowledged his need for dependence and openness. As a result, he was brought into a caring community where he could receive the support he needed. People who loved him walked alongside him on his difficult journey. And so did God.

Confession has the same results in our lives. When we agree with God and speak the truth, we unleash great power for good in ourselves and in those to whom we confess.

Words are important to God. He created the world with the spoken word, and Jesus is the Word of God made flesh. In ways we can only imagine, God has given power to words, and that power is released when we speak the truth—the truth about ourselves as well as about God.

Notes

1. W. E. Vine, *Expository Dictionary of New Testament Words* (Grand Rapids, Mich.: Zondervan, 1952), s.v. "confess."

START TODAY!

How to Speak the Truth

- Agree with God about what he says is true and right
- Agree with God about what he says is wrong
- Speak the truth to God about what you have done wrong
- Speak the truth to another person about what you have done wrong
- Speak the truth about what others have done to you without denying, avoiding, or minimizing
- Express your feelings honestly
- Put your vague sense of guilt into words that express your sins
- Pray for one another as you hear their confessions and they hear yours
- Stop keeping secrets from God
- Worship God in spirit and in truth

BIBLICAL EXAMPLE

David's confession

BIBLE VERSE

James 5:16: "Confess your sins to each other and pray for each other so that you may be healed."

Chapter 4
Take Responsibility

Each one should carry his own load.

Galatians 6:5, NIV

If you do not carry your own cross and follow me,
you cannot be my disciple.

Luke 14:27

PETER had been with Jesus since the beginning of Jesus'
ministry. In fact, Peter was one of the first men Jesus called
to follow him. One day Peter was casting his nets on the Sea
of Galilee, trying to catch fish. The next day he was learning
from Jesus how to "fish" for human souls. The change happened that fast. Perhaps Peter had heard about Jesus and
was eager to learn more from him. Or maybe he was just
tired of fishing and wanted a change in routine. Fishing was
hard work. The nets were heavy. The sea was dangerous.
The weather was erratic. The catch was unpredictable. Fishing was a difficult way to make a living.

We don't know for sure what Peter's motive was for following Jesus, but we do know that he did not hesitate when
Jesus called him. He immediately dropped his nets and followed.

Based on the kind of person Peter became later in life,

we might conclude that his motive was a noble one: his eagerness to learn about Jesus. But from what we know about his early life, the more logical conclusion is that Peter just wanted change. He was impulsive. He was quick-tempered. He was dramatic. Peter didn't spend a lot of time thinking before acting. He followed his instincts. This characteristic served him well in his initial decision to follow Jesus, but it got him into a lot of trouble before he learned to use it for good.

When Jesus walked on the water, Peter was the only disciple courageous enough to try it himself. But no sooner had he stepped out of the boat than a gust of wind whisked away his faith and a wave of doubt nearly pulled him under. When Jesus was arrested on the Mount of Olives, Peter drew his sword and slashed off the ear of the high priest's servant. Jesus stopped him, saying, "No more of this." And he put the ear back in place. When Jesus tried to warn Peter about the temptations he would soon face, Peter argued, assuring Jesus that he loved him so much he would die for him. But before dawn the next day, Peter denied Jesus three times. Emotional, impetuous, and passionate Peter started things he couldn't finish, created problems he couldn't solve, and made promises he couldn't keep. Yet Jesus chose him, loved him, redeemed him, and used him.

Jesus did this not by changing Peter's personality but by changing Peter's heart. Jesus didn't make Peter less passionate; he just changed what he was passionate about. In other words, Jesus *redeemed* Peter. He turned Peter's life around and used it for good. And that's exactly what Jesus wants to do in each of our lives. The apostle Paul addressed this issue in his letter to the Ephesian church:

> Since you have heard about Jesus and have learned the truth that comes from him, throw off your old sinful nature

and your former way of life, which is corrupted by lust and deception. Instead, let the Spirit renew your thoughts and attitudes. Put on your new nature, created to be like God—truly righteous and holy.   Ephesians 4:21-24

Before we can throw off our old sinful nature and former way of life, we first have to identify what they are. Once we recognize our flaws and admit our weaknesses, we can take responsibility for ourselves by avoiding situations in which we are likely to sin.

None of us has a choice as to which traits and tendencies we inherit, but we can choose what we do with them. We can either spend our time comparing them to those belonging to others—a habit that leads either to envy and pouting or to pride and self-sufficiency—or we can cooperate with God as he uses them for good in his Kingdom.

Taking responsibility for the characteristics we inherit from our earthly parents means placing them all under the power and authority of our heavenly parent—God—and allowing him to redeem them for his use.

Taking Responsibility for Our Emotions

Emotions are the animating force within us. They energize and motivate us. They are the desires that propel us forward and the forces that hold us back. It is important, therefore, that we bring them into alignment with our beliefs. If we neglect to do this, we end up working against ourselves; we do things we believe are wrong and we fail to do things we believe are right. This results first in guilt, then in numbness. We cannot live in conflict with ourselves indefinitely, so eventually we change either our behavior or our beliefs.

Unfortunately, the trend in our culture is to change beliefs. That is why so many people today claim that certain behaviors are "lifestyle choices," not sin. Unwilling to change their behavior and unable to live in conflict, they change what they think is true to match what they want to do. In the long run, however, this does not work because emotions are fickle—what we *want* changes with the wind.

Both fear and anger are motivating emotions, but they are at opposite ends of the motivational scale. Fear paralyzes us and anger incites us. Fear keeps us from doing what is right; anger causes us to do what is wrong.

Amy, for example, was fearful about handling her finances. She avoided balancing her checkbook and put off paying bills. The reason for her fear was legitimate: she didn't have the money to pay all of her bills. But denial and avoidance were not the solution. By allowing fear to paralyze her, Amy allowed the problem to get worse.

Whenever we get stuck in a problem, fear is the most likely cause. And fear is an indication that it's time to take responsibility for an area of life that is out of control. In this case, bill paying was Amy's apparent fear but not the real one; her real fear was having to face up to the truth that she was living beyond her means. Once she had identified the fear, it was then easy to see that the solution was not a better system of bill paying. The solution for Amy was to cut back on expenditures, find a higher-paying job, or ask for a raise—in other words, take responsibility.

People who live at the opposite end of the motivating scale of emotions are those who react violently to the smallest incidents. They are the people we describe as having a short fuse; the smallest spark of conflict sets them ablaze. Sometimes excessive anger is the fuel that keeps them moving. Sometimes it is a tool to control others. And sometimes it is a deep frustration, disappointment, or betrayal that has turned into hatred. A quick temper or ongoing anger is a warning that it's time to face some unresolved problem or to develop a weak area of our character.

One aspect of taking responsibility for our feelings is to not blame others for our own inappropriate responses. Other people can indeed hurt us, but they can't *make* us lash out in anger. When we take responsibility for our emotions, we acknowledge what others have done to us, but we stop short of blaming them for our inappropriate responses, realizing that their wrongdoing doesn't require us to react inappropriately. We do not excuse or condone their hurtful behavior, but neither do we use it as an excuse for our own. Those who do so will continue to consider themselves victims and thus will feel justified in compounding the damage. Taking responsibility for our reactions frees us from this horrible cycle of victimization.

Whenever our emotional reaction to an event is out of proportion to its seriousness—either too high or too low—it is evidence that our mind and emotions are out of sync.

It is important for us to remember that emotions that make us feel bad are not necessarily bad emotions. Grief, for example, is an appropriate response to the loss of something good, and remorse is a healthy response to sin. While tears of regret do not feel good, it is nevertheless good for us to experience the pain our actions have caused others and ourselves.

Part of taking responsibility for our emotions is to be willing to tolerate bad feelings. This is not a popular idea. People prefer to anesthetize bad feelings with mood-altering drugs or to indulge in some unhealthy but exhilarating behavior to hide them.

Tears cleanse the soul. They seep into the cracks and wash away stubborn bitterness and resentment. They also put us in touch with Jesus, our High Priest, who identifies with us in suffering and grief.

> This High Priest of ours understands our weaknesses, for he
> faced all of the same testings we do, yet he did not sin. So
> let us come boldly to the throne of our gracious God. There
> we will receive his mercy, and we will find grace to help us
> when we need it most.   Hebrews 4:15-16

In the ancient Hebrew religion, the high priest repre-
sented the sin of all the Hebrew people when he approached
God. Jesus, though without sin, is known as the man of sor-
rows (see Isaiah 53:3-5). We cannot truly identify ourselves
with Jesus until we have experienced grief over sin—grief
that motivates us to turn our backs on sin and begin walking in a new direction. This is called repentance.

Emotions are a gift from God. Sometimes they carry us
to heights of happiness. Other times they drag us into the
depths of despair. But when we stop denying them and
begin accepting them, examining them, processing them,
and expressing them openly and honestly, they can be a cat-
alyst for spiritual renewal.

Taking Responsibility for Our Minds

God calls his people to love him with heart, soul, *mind,* and
strength. Each of us is responsible to study God's Word, to
handle his truth accurately, and to participate with him in
the renewing of our minds: "Do not conform any longer to
the pattern of this world, but be transformed by the renewing of your mind" (Romans 12:2, NIV).

It is not always easy to identify patterns of worldly
thinking. They become so familiar to us that we seldom
even think of them as worldly. One example of a worldly
thought pattern that we seldom question is the idea that
people over the age of seventeen can fill their minds with
garbage and remain mentally unpolluted. While it may be
true that people of a certain age ought to have enough
maturity not to imitate the behavior they see in movies or

on television, it is faulty to assume that people of any age can remain unaffected by what they see or hear. Just because we are adults doesn't mean that our brains have become disengaged from our senses. What we see and hear *does* affect how we think and behave. And just because we have the legal right to participate in certain activities does not mean that we have the moral right to do so.

What we put into our minds via our senses determines whether we will be conformed to the world or transformed into the likeness of Christ. We transform our minds by filling them with God's Word; we pollute our minds by filling them with images and messages that contradict God.

Even that, however, is too simplistic. Remaining close to Jesus does not guarantee clear thinking. Remember Peter. Even after living day in and day out with Jesus, witnessing many of his miracles, and hearing many of his sermons, Peter still had foggy thinking. He still had his own ideas as to what Jesus should do and how he should get it done. And know-it-all Peter didn't hesitate to argue with Jesus when he didn't like what he heard him preaching.

When Jesus started talking about his need to suffer rejection and death, Peter took him aside to speak privately to him. The Jewish people were awaiting a political messiah, a king to replace David on the throne, and just moments earlier Peter had affirmed that he believed Jesus was this long-awaited ruler. So who can blame Peter for being confused when Jesus immediately thereafter started talking about suffering and death? Peter may have thought Jesus was just discouraged and in need of a pep talk. But Jesus did not appreciate Peter's misguided attempt to help, and he expressed his displeasure in rather blunt language: "Get away from me, Satan!" he said. "You are seeing things merely from a human point of view, not from God's" (see Mark 8:31-33).

This shows how dangerous it is to assume that we know the mind of God simply because we read the Word of God. Despite eating, sleeping, and walking alongside the Word of God incarnate, Peter still had in mind "the things of men."

It is impossible for me to exaggerate our need for transformed minds, and it is essential that I stress the danger of assuming that the process in us is complete. Our minds are in need of ongoing renewal. We must accept the responsibility to renew our minds daily through prayer and meditation on God's Word and to stand guard against the polluting influences of the world that assault our senses at every turn.

Taking Responsibility for Our Bodies

Michael has not had a drink of alcohol in ten years. He doesn't make a big deal about being a teetotaler, but he doesn't try to hide it either. He avoids going into bars even if the people he is with go in while waiting to be seated at a restaurant.

Michael has taken responsibility for his weakness for alcohol and has learned not to take risks in that area. When asked about his avoidance of liquor, he quotes a friend, who once warned him: "Never say you've gotten strong enough to beat alcohol. Alcohol is always in the next room, working out."

Clinical evidence reveals that some people are born with characteristics predisposing them toward behavior that is likely to result in sin.[1] Some people, for example, are particularly vulnerable to the effects of drugs and alcohol, and they become addicted very easily. This predisposition, however, is not an excuse for drug addiction and alcoholism; rather it is a reason (and a warning!) to avoid using drugs and alcohol.

God gives each of us the responsibility of caring for our bodies, keeping in mind that they are his temple. That means we should use our bodies only in ways that honor him:

> God's will is for you to be holy, so stay away from all sexual sin. Then each of you will control his own body and live in holiness and honor—not in lustful passion like the pagans who do not know God and his ways.   1 Thessalonians 4:3-5

Know our weaknesses

All of us have inherent weaknesses that make us vulnerable to particular kinds of sin. What is dangerous for a person like Michael may be harmless to someone else. But we must all accept responsibility for our own evil desires and guard against them. We sometimes think that all temptation exists outside ourselves, but this is not true. At least some of it is always with us. As James 1:14-16 says, "Temptation comes from our own desires, which entice us and drag us away. These desires give birth to sinful actions. And when sin is allowed to grow, it gives birth to death. So don't be misled."

Part of taking responsibility for our own evil desires is to identify and avoid locations, situations, or people that trigger temptation. These may include familiar hangouts where we have previously fallen into sin. This is not as easy as it sounds. Often these places seem innocuous—and sometimes they are the very places we go to find comfort—or to escape discomfort. For example, a person who uses sleep as an escape from stress ought to stay away from overstuffed chairs and couches, where the need for a short nap may end in a wasted day. The man who uses food to make himself feel good ought to avoid the local donut shop, where a familiar pleasure quickly becomes an episode of self-indulgence and ends in regret and self-loathing. And the woman who spends too much money ought to avoid the mall.

It is essential that we know ourselves and our weaknesses well enough to know what is dangerous, what is harmless, and what is simply a waste of time. We can avoid a lot of grief and pain simply by avoiding places that draw us into sensuality and self-gratification.

Accept our limitations

If you have grown to an adult height of four feet and eleven inches, accept that you probably won't get any taller. And if you have a handicap or disability, accept that you can't do everything, but don't let that keep you from doing *something*. If we use what we *can't* do as an excuse for not doing what we *can* do, we have failed to take responsibility for our bodies.

Despite being unable to hear, see, or speak, Helen Keller accomplished tremendous things. She did so because she accepted her limitations but did not exaggerate them. She expressed such an attitude in this statement: "I am only one; but still I am one. I cannot do everything, but still I can do something. I will not refuse to do the something I can do."

Given your physical limitations, what can you do and do well? That is what you are responsible to do.

Follow God's moral laws

God has set out clear moral laws in his Word. They are encapsulated in the Ten Commandments, developed in the Sermon on the Mount, summarized in the Golden Rule, and expounded on throughout the Bible. Anyone who has tried to follow them learns quickly that to do so is humanly impossible. Part of taking responsibility for our humanity is accepting that we cannot keep God's law. However, this realization is meant to lead us to Christ, who not only kept the law but is himself the embodiment of the law. Through him we are aligned with God's code of moral conduct. No mere human does it perfectly, but that is to be our aim. Paul put it this way: "So whether we are here in this body or away from this body, our goal is to please him" (2 Corinthians 5:9).

One day each of us will stand before Christ and give account of what we have done with our body. Therefore, while acknowledging that we are never going to be perfect in this life, we must, nevertheless, continually aim to please God in our conduct.

Taking Responsibility for Our Spirits

Each of us determines where we will spend eternity by choosing whether or not to accept the salvation offered to us by God and paid for with the life, death, and resurrection of Jesus. After we receive salvation, we are to continue allowing God to work in our lives.

> Dear friends, you always followed my instructions when I was with you. And now that I am away, it is even more important. Work hard to show the results of your salvation, obeying God with deep reverence and fear. For God is working in you, giving you the desire and the power to do what pleases him. Do everything without complaining and arguing, so that no one can criticize you. Live clean, innocent lives as children of God, shining like bright lights in a world full of crooked and perverse people. Philippians 2:12-15

Through worship

The only activity practiced by the church today that will continue throughout eternity is worship. Yet we seldom teach anything about it. We teach people how to get along with one another, we teach them how to evangelize and how to pray, and we teach them about the Bible. But rarely does a church teach its people how to worship. Apparently we assume it is just one of those things that happens when everything else is right. But that may be a dangerous assumption. As early as the second generation of humans there arose a problem concerning worship.

> Abel became a shepherd, while Cain cultivated the ground. When it was time for the harvest, Cain presented some of his crops as a gift to the LORD. Abel also brought a gift—the best of the firstborn lambs from his flock. The LORD accepted Abel and his gift, but he did not accept Cain and his gift. Genesis 4:2-5

As Cain discovered, it is unwise to assume that almighty God is happy with whatever we feel like giving him. God is seeking those who will worship him in spirit and in truth, and that means knowing him well enough to know what he wants and loving him enough to actually give it.

Through the exercise of spiritual gifts

God gives each believer spiritual gifts to use in building up the church and to enhance his or her own spiritual development. We are responsible to identify our spiritual gifts and use them for good. Peter writes,

> God has given each of you a gift from his great variety of spiritual gifts. Use them well to serve one another. Do you have the gift of speaking? Then speak as though God himself were speaking through you. Do you have the gift of helping others? Do it with all the strength and energy that God supplies. 1 Peter 4:10-11

The Bible expounds on spiritual gifts in several places. The most extensive passages are Romans 12 and 1 Corinthians 12, but Ephesians 4 mentions several as well. Here is how Scripture lists them:

From Romans 12: prophesying, serving, teaching, encouraging, giving, leading, showing mercy. *From 1 Corinthians 12:* wisdom, knowledge, faith, healing, miracles, prophecy, discernment, helping, administration, tongues, interpretation of tongues. *From Ephesians 4:* apostles, evangelists, pastors, and teachers.

In the New Testament the apostle Paul uses the metaphor of a body to describe believers and their purpose. Every believer is a part of Christ's body, he explains, and God assigns and equips each person to accomplish a unique function in that body.

Often we think of spiritual gifts as strictly a New Testament phenomenon, given by God at about the same time he sent the Holy Spirit to indwell believers. But God granted spiritual gifts to his people as early as the time of Moses. In the account of the Exodus we read,

> Then the LORD said to Moses, "Look, I have specifically chosen Bezalel son of Uri, grandson of Hur, of the tribe of Judah. I have filled him with the Spirit of God, giving him great wisdom, ability, and expertise in all kinds of crafts. He is a master craftsman, expert in working with gold, silver, and bronze. He is skilled in engraving and mounting gemstones and in carving wood. He is a master at every craft!"
>
> Exodus 31:1-5

God gives each believer special abilities to use in accomplishing his work in the world. Just as each part of a machine is designed to perform a certain function as part of a larger task, each member of God's royal family has a special task to perform for his Kingdom.

Knowing our spiritual gifts is important because it enables us to make wise choices about how to use our time, talent, and financial resources most effectively for the Kingdom of God. And using our gifts is important because it results in fulfillment that comes only from having accomplished the things God has called us to do.

People often feel neglected and abandoned by God. They feel inadequate, useless, and unworthy. But beneath all of that negative emotion is a gift (or two or three) from God. When we accept that gift and use it to strengthen the church, many of our negative feelings vanish. Life offers no greater satisfaction than that of using our experiences, gifts, and even our sufferings for the good of others. To help, comfort, encourage, and guide another person and to realize that we are the one person on earth whom God has prepared and equipped to do so, is to find true fulfillment.

One of the joys of discovering our spiritual gifts is learning that the things we have the most passion for are usually the areas in which we are most gifted.

Even if we are unsure whether or not a particular talent is a spiritual gift, we are well within the boundaries of God's will to use it in helping others in the body of Christ and in taking God's good news to those outside.

We can determine our spiritual gifts in a number of ways: Bible study and prayer, personal reflection, and the counsel of spiritually mature people who have observed us in various situations. Sometimes a spiritual gift comes so naturally that we assume everyone is born with it. When people express surprise as to how well we performed a particular task or responded in a specific situation, they are giving an important clue as to our spiritual giftedness.

Another way to determine spiritual gifts is by taking a spiritual gifts inventory test. These are similar to personality tests, and they are available in books, on the Internet, or from several organizations.

Paul told the believers at Corinth to diligently seek spiritual gifts, but he emphasized that the overriding principle governing the practice of all of them is love:

If I could speak all the languages of earth and of angels, but didn't love others, I would only be a noisy gong or a clanging cymbal. If I had the gift of prophecy, and if I understood all of God's secret plans and possessed all knowledge, and if I had such faith that I could move mountains, but didn't love others, I would be nothing. If I gave everything I have to the poor and even sacrificed my body, I could boast about it; but if I didn't love others, I would have gained nothing.

1 Corinthians 13:1-3

Taking Responsibility for Our Experiences

Every person alive experiences pain. In our fallen world, evil is a painful reality. While God is not the author of evil, he allows it to touch our lives for reasons we cannot understand.

Technically speaking, David Ring was born dead. Quick-acting medical personnel were able to get him breathing, but oxygen deprivation left him with cerebral palsy. He suffers from a speech impediment, hands that don't cooperate, and a limp. As if that wasn't enough adversity for one person, both his parents died by the time he was fourteen years old, and his hemophiliac brothers subsequently died of AIDS.

David's remaining family members feared that he would never have a normal life because they assumed he would never marry, have children, drive a car, earn a living, or take care of himself.

As a young teenager, David surrendered his life and condition to God and came to see his disability as a gift. Once he accepted his circumstances as being chosen for him by God, he began moving forward. Today he is married, has four beautiful children, drives a car, and speaks to more than 250 audiences a year. At his speaking engagements he sells T-shirts bearing the slogan "Don't Whine—SHINE!"

David Ring has taken responsibility for his life—the

bad, the difficult, and the wonderful—and he continues to celebrate the difference he is able to make in the lives of other people.

When people wrestle with difficult life experiences, the *why* question often gets in the way. One of David Ring's axioms is, "Don't ask God *why*. Ask *what*. *What* do you want me to do with this?"

In counseling, the *why* question is probably the biggest barrier to spiritual and emotional growth. There simply is no satisfying answer to it. *Why* stops spiritual progress whereas *what* moves it along. When we ask "What can I do with this difficulty?" our focus changes from looking back to what was and what might have been to looking forward to what is and what is to be.

In life, people are prone to experience all manner of distress. If we were to categorize them, the list would look like this:

Natural wrongs

Birth defects, disease, and tragedies that cannot be traced to any human cause (e.g., hurricanes, volcanoes, and floods). Although the latter may be described as "acts of God" by insurance companies, they are in fact examples of events that strike both the just and the unjust without differentiation.

Inadvertent wrongs

Accidents and all other unintentional injury or damage for which it is unreasonable to blame anyone.

Self-inflicted wrongs

The misuse of drugs, alcohol, food, or anything else that damages a person's mind, body, or emotions. This category also includes the failure to stay out of dangerous relationships and situations.

Intentional wrongs

Physical injury, emotional harm, financial damage, or any other impairment resulting from another person's immoral, unethical, or illegal conduct.

When something bad happens, we have three choices: We can pretend it didn't happen (which is to abdicate responsibility). We can host a pity party for ourselves (but the guests eventually will get bored and go on to someone with a more tragic story). Or we can acknowledge God's right to allow in our lives whatever circumstances will make us the most useful to him.

Unwelcome as they are, problems can stimulate spiritual growth. They show where change is needed, and they deepen our character when we seek biblical solutions to them. Problems can cause us to pray as nothing else can. They change our hearts from within and give us more compassion for others.

An important part of taking responsibility for our lives is to admit the part we have played in creating our problems and to assume responsibility for doing whatever we can to solve them.

Taking Responsibility for Our Relationships

Natural disasters are impossible to avoid. Accidents are inevitable. And we have no choice regarding our family of origin. Right there we have three major areas of potential trouble over which we have no control. You would think that would be enough for anyone. But most of us insist on adding to the list by making foolish choices regarding friends (and sometimes even marriage partners, but that's another book). A common tendency in choosing friends is to pick people who make us feel good about ourselves. We gravitate toward those who "accept us as we are" (even though it's usually because they don't want any pressure put on them to get any better). But how much better it is to spend time with people who inspire us to become better than we are.

Choose friends wisely

The company we keep can make the difference between moving toward spiritual renewal and transformation or moving backward into sin and self-destruction. As the Bible warns, "Bad company corrupts good character" (1 Corinthians 15:33).

The book of Proverbs, on the other hand, offers this wisdom: "As iron sharpens iron, so a friend sharpens a friend" (27:17). We ought to be spending time with people who will sharpen our thinking, support us with prayer, and encourage us with their godly behavior.

Close friends ought to have a positive outlook and an uplifting attitude. Christian or not, people who are always complaining and seeing the negative side of things are an emotional drain. The same is true of one-sided friendships where the focus is always on the other person's problems.

People who are working through their problems without self-pity or bitterness can nurture our growth and become good friends. Although it can be good to get input from people who struggle with the same temptations we do, those with whom we associate closely should have a history of victory over the temptation, not just a mound of good intentions.

We all need other people, but we don't need people who will drag us into despair and hopelessness. We need people who will encourage us, confront us, and continually nudge us in the right direction.

Make peace quickly

Relationships are a lot easier when everyone's best interest is the same. But there comes a time in every relationship when what is best for one person conflicts with what is best for the other. If the relationship has been relatively smooth, the two people may be caught off guard when this happens. In this kind of situation, serious damage can be done if either party assumes that his or her best interest has ultimate priority. Maturity is essential at such times because the people involved need to look ahead, focus on the common (or higher) goal, and submit themselves to the strategy that will help them reach it.

Unfortunately, no one does this perfectly or consistently. It is human nature to think that our own needs are most important and so we manipulate, deceive, and strong-arm our way through life, oblivious or insensitive to the trouble or hurt we are causing others.

We all do this, and some of us do it habitually. But Jesus says not to come to God until our relationships with others are right: "If you are presenting a sacrifice at the altar in the Temple and you suddenly remember that someone has something against you, leave your sacrifice there at the altar. Go and be reconciled to that person. Then come and offer your sacrifice to God" (Matthew 5:23-24).

Jesus didn't mention who was to blame when he gave these instructions. He simply said fix it. Scripture gives specific directions for resolving differences within the family of faith (see Matthew 18:15-20). Whenever there is something amiss between ourselves and another person, it is our responsibility to do whatever we can to make it right.

Taking Responsibility for Our Future
As one popular idiom says, "If you keep on doin' what you've always been doin', you're goin' to keep on gettin' what you've been gettin'." Stated another way, if we want to avoid the same old results, we need to avoid the same old behaviors.

Regardless of what we have done in the past, God has something better for us to do in the future. And the something better that God has in mind for each of us is a holy life. When we begin a personal relationship with Jesus Christ, we remain the same person but we change direction. Instead of following our own desires, we pursue God's. Instead of living to accumulate the wealth of this earthly kingdom, we pursue the riches of God's spiritual Kingdom.

> By his divine power, God has given us everything we need for living a godly life. We have received all of this by coming to know him, the one who called us to himself by means of his marvelous glory and excellence. And because of his glory and excellence, he has given us great and precious promises. These are the promises that enable you to share his divine nature and escape the world's corruption caused by human desires. 2 Peter 1:3-4

Turning *toward* God is the same as turning away from all that is ungodly. Eventually this makes us uncomfortable with anything that is out of sync with God's will.

For those seeking spiritual renewal, the goal is not comfort but growth. The familiar illustration of the oyster makes an important point here. The oyster feels a lot of discomfort when a grain of sand slips between its two protective shells and lodges in its tender flesh. But the poor oyster is handicapped and disadvantaged. He has no fingers or tweezers with which to remove the irritating grit. So, since he can't get rid of the aggravation, he makes the best of it. He begins coating the grit with a smooth surface until it no longer irritates him.

We all know the result of the oyster's efforts: a pearl. A simple object, yet beautiful in its smooth, round whiteness. A small object, yet valuable because of its scarcity. Most people who use this illustration focus on the result of the irritation—the pearl. But what about the oyster? Is a pearl of any value to him? No. Can an oyster appreciate the beauty of a pearl? No. The poor oyster suffers all the discomfort and does all the work, but all he gets for his trouble is a little relief from his misery. Someone he doesn't even know from a world he's never been a part of comes along and gets the reward for his labor. It hardly seems fair.

But that's how God's economy works. Each of us needs to accept the possibility that the only benefit we'll get from the work we do on ourselves is relief from the things that irritate us. But that is no small advantage. Think about some of the ways wholesome habits reduce or eliminate the irritations that cause stress in our lives. For example,

- Working hard reduces the likelihood of financial stress.
- Being dependable eliminates the stress of having to make excuses.
- Taking care of our bodies reduces the likelihood of stress due to sickness and disease.
- Being a faithful spouse and/or friend reduces the possibility of stress due to a broken relationship.
- Being honest eliminates the stress of being caught (or the fear that we will be) in our lies.
- Staying in touch with God through Bible reading and prayer reduces the stress of confusion that comes when we start believing the world's value system.

Good habits cannot remove all irritations, but they can prevent many of them and bring relief from many others. However, the biggest value of our efforts may never be known to us. In fact, God's purpose in having us work through an irritation may be for the good of someone we don't know and don't even care about.

When we have the faith and motivation to do good

under those conditions, we are being spiritually renewed. And when we take responsibility for the assorted choices we've made in life, we discover that our past failures do not prevent us from developing a deep and loving relationship with God. When we finally acknowledge our waywardness rather than rationalize it, Jesus hands us a clean slate.

The apostle Peter is a great example of this. He denied Jesus when Jesus needed him most. He proved himself a traitor to the Savior of the universe. And then he plunged into depression as he realized the depths of his depravity.

Did Jesus forsake Peter for his betrayal? No. Did he spurn him for his rejection? No. Did he despise him for his weakness? No. Quite the opposite in fact.

Instead of chiding Peter, Jesus commissioned him: "Feed my lambs." Instead of forsaking Peter, Jesus empowered him: "Take care of my sheep." Instead of relieving Peter of responsibility, Jesus entrusted him with more: "Feed my sheep."

Peter followed Jesus, then failed him. Peter grieved over his sin, then received restoration. Peter stopped lying to save his life, then lost his life for the sake of truth. By taking responsibility for his life, brash, impetuous Peter experienced spiritual renewal and became a brave and impassioned follower of Jesus.

When we take responsibility for all that we are, for all that we have done, and for all that God wants us to become, we are participating with him in his grand and glorious plan—the redemption of all creation.

Notes

1. See discussion in *Hand-Me-Down Genes and Second-Hand Emotions*, Stephen Arterburn (Simon & Schuster, 1994).

START TODAY!

How to Take Responsibility

- Know what responsibilities God expects you to carry and then carry them out
- Examine your own spiritual "backpack" and sort it out
- Take responsibility for your God-given roles
- Take responsibility for your actions and attitudes
- Keep your commitments and promises
- Unload that which God does not intend you to carry
- Face your problems rather than try to escape them
- Experience your emotions and grieve your losses instead of pretending you have none
- Refuse to blame others for your sinful reactions to life
- Accept God's provision for salvation

BIBLICAL EXAMPLE

Peter's denial of Jesus and subsequent ministry

BIBLE VERSE

Galatians 6:5: "Each one should carry his own load" (NIV).

Chapter 5

Grieve, Forgive, and Let Go

If you forgive those who sin against you,
your heavenly Father will forgive you.
But if you refuse to forgive others,
your Father will not forgive your sins.

Matthew 6:14-15

JOSEPH was the pride and joy of his father. Though Jacob had ten other sons, he favored Joseph, the one born to him in his old age. Jacob never bothered to hide his special feelings—not even from his other sons. In fact, he expressed his favoritism blatantly and visibly by having an expensive coat made especially for Joseph.

This did not go unnoticed by the older brothers, and they began to resent their spoiled young sibling. Joseph, who was either oblivious to their resentment or insensitive to it, made it worse by bragging to his brothers about his dreams that he would one day rule over them. In one dream, his brothers' sheaves of grain bowed down to his. In another dream, the sun, moon, and eleven stars bowed down to him.

Eventually, Joseph's vivid dreams and their father's favoritism so infuriated the brothers that they plotted Joseph's death. While trying to decide the best way to accomplish it, they spotted a caravan of spice traders on the way to Egypt. Instead of killing Joseph, they decided to sell him as a slave. They said good riddance to their dreaming, scheming brother and made up a story to tell their father about his favorite son's tragic fate.

So much for dreams of greatness. At age seventeen, Joseph became a slave in Egypt, then a prisoner in a rank dungeon for a crime he did not commit. The situation provided Joseph with plenty of raw material for resentment. But it also gave him plenty of time to think about his life and what he had done. Somewhere along the way, Joseph made a choice. He decided to forgive his brothers. Eventually God fulfilled the promise he had conveyed through dreams to the brash young man, but not before refining Joseph's character through forgiveness.

The Importance of Forgiveness

Forgiveness is something all of us want to receive but most of us hesitate to give. Jesus made it clear, however, that we can't have it without giving it. "If you forgive those who sin against you, your heavenly Father will forgive you. But if you refuse to forgive others, your Father will not forgive your sins" (Matthew 6:14-15). These words allow no room for doubt or discussion. Forgiveness flows two ways. We cannot separate *receiving* forgiveness from *extending* forgiveness.

Forgiveness is at the core of emotional well-being. It is fair to say that unforgiving people are emotionally sick. Their bitterness is a disease of the spirit, and it is inevitable that the unforgiving person eventually will experience physical illness as well. Anger causes surges of adrenaline and secretes other powerful chemicals that attack the body. The stress we carry when we refuse to give or receive forgiveness affects our hearts, minds, and bodies. To make matters worse, both rage and depression contribute to obsessive behaviors such as overeating, workaholism, overspending, and even addictions to pornography and mood-altering drugs. We cannot rid ourselves of emotional pain and its side effects unless we are willing to forgive.

Unresolved anger keeps us from moving forward because it locks us in a time machine, frozen on the exact moment when a particular offense occurred. Fear of further injury makes us unwilling to move to new levels of relationship, not only with those who have hurt us but with anyone who represents a similar threat.

Furthermore, if we allow unforgiveness to continue, we are likely to experience depression, bitterness, or both. Yet more important than any of these concerns is the most serious consideration of all—the spiritual consequence of unforgiveness: alienation from God.

Forgiveness cannot begin until we admit our own failures. If we cannot do that much, we can neither give nor receive forgiveness. We cannot receive forgiveness without acknowledging our need for it, and we cannot extend forgiveness without admitting that because of our own imperfect condition we have no right to withhold forgiveness from anyone else. For Christians, forgiveness is nonnegotiable; it is the very essence of our faith.

Receiving Forgiveness

Even though we all want to be forgiven, pride often stands in the way of asking for it. We would rather carry the guilt than admit our failure. I was one of those people. By the time I reached my early twenties, I had filled my life with rebellion and self-centeredness. I was well on my way down the highway of self-destruction. Despite many attempts to turn my life around, none had produced lasting change. Steeped in sin and secrecy, I struggled to be better, only to find myself deeper in despair, suffering at my own hands.

After two years of college, I was aware of how horribly I had messed up my life, and my hopes of changing were all but gone. I was desperate enough to try anything, so when my parents offered to pay my way to a popular Christian conference, I went, hoping that something would make a difference. I knew that toward the end of the weeklong convention an assignment would be given that I would, under no circumstances, complete. I hoped, however, that I could get enough out of the rest of the seminar to change the course of my life.

The seminar went well, and I started to feel a slight bit of hope, even though "the assignment" still loomed over me. I thought of a few excuses to not show up on the night it would be given, but I finally dragged myself there. That evening I met a beautiful Christian girl named Cindy. I imagined how wonderful it would be to have a friend like her, but I did not consider myself worthy to even think such a thing. However, meeting her made me even more aware of the benefits of turning my life around. That night I heard the conference leader talk about being able to look everyone in the eye and feel no shame. It seemed like an impossible dream. Then came the dreaded assignment: write, call, or talk to every person I had ever hurt and ask each one to forgive me.

The reason I could never do such a thing was because I had never acknowledged to anyone that I did anything wrong. My life was "perfect." No one knew I was suffering. Completing this task would require at least five things I could not imagine myself ever doing: surrendering my will to God; admitting the wrong I had done without rationalizing it; humbling myself to acknowledge the seriousness of what I had done; taking responsibility to make restitution wherever I could; asking people to give me something I could not give myself—their forgiveness.

I knew this plan had the potential to completely transform my attitude, my actions, and my life. But I would not do it! Though I was hurting, I was still full of pride. Then the speaker began to list other benefits:

- Relief from guilt over things I could not undo
- Emotional strength and spiritual renewal
- Intimacy with God

Intimacy with God seemed like a remote possibility, but it was the hope that kept me going. By the end of the evening, I had started my list of people to contact. I put on the list anyone I could think of who had any reason to hold a grudge against me. If I questioned whether the offense was too great to be forgiven, I wrote it down anyway. The list was long and my sorrow deep over the many people I had hurt in selfish attempts to make myself feel good.

When I had finished the list, I began making the contacts. Each one brought a flood of tears and a rush of healing. No person turned me away. Everyone was grateful for the call, many adding how they had contributed to the problem. Burden by burden, I was freed from years of guilt and shame. Joy and hope replaced my heavy spirit.

One particularly difficult call was to a religion professor whose tests I had cheated on. Imagine cheating on a Bible test! Can it get any dumber than that? I confessed to the professor, requested his forgiveness, and asked how I might make restitution. He said I should take the tests again. I swallowed hard, took a deep breath, and agreed to his plan. It was not a pleasant consequence, but I now have an honest grade and a clear conscience.

To this day I still write letters and ask forgiveness when the Holy Spirit pricks my conscience. I know I have missed some people, but I try to keep my accounts current. I also try to live in such a way that I'll not have to ask forgiveness from too many people. The memory of this exercise keeps me from drifting back into old behavior patterns.

The thought of talking to people we have wronged is frightening! Apologies are not easy. How much more difficult it is to actually verbalize the wrongs and offer restitution. But we cannot avoid doing it. This humbling exercise helps us experience the reality of forgiveness. Unless we feel some of the pain we have caused others, we won't appreciate the value of offering forgiveness nor comprehend our need for receiving it.

Start by making a list of the people you have hurt and the wrongs you have done. Ask the Holy Spirit to bring to mind the names of people who ought to be on the list. When your list is complete, discuss it with a trusted friend or counselor who can pray with you, encourage you, and counsel you as you work to make things right.

One important consideration when making amends is the potential for adding injury. For example, a letter or phone call that might reveal a past affair to a person's spouse could cause more problems than it resolves. Making restitution when it has the potential to add hurt is a selfish act. The purpose of making amends is not to make ourselves feel better, especially at the expense of others; it's to obey Jesus and change the direction of our lives. Use this paraphrase of the Golden Rule when seeking forgiveness: *Don't intrude on the life of someone you've hurt, even to make restitution, if you wouldn't want the person to do the same to you under the same circumstances.*

As you prepare for this task, here are some things you need to be ready to do:

- Repay money.
- Restore material objects you've acquired through theft, family dispute, or misunderstanding.

- Admit to your ex-spouse your share of blame for the divorce.
- Visit a therapist with the wronged party.
- Call estranged parents, children, or other relatives.
- Recant gossip you've spread.
- Restart your marriage at ground zero with a new commitment, new boundaries, and a new vision for the future.

Whatever it is, don't be surprised that it's difficult. If it were easy, you probably would have done it before now. But it must be done, not only for the sake of those you injured but for your own spiritual well-being.

Extending Forgiveness

Emotional pain never dies a natural death, and we can't kill it by burying it. If we try to bury pain while it is still alive, it will kick and scream until we acknowledge it, feel it, and put it behind us through forgiveness. We can put it out of our minds through denial, but the only way to get it out of our hearts is through forgiveness.

Unexpressed grief festers and swells, waiting to erupt. It may explode in uncontrollable rage, gush out in unstoppable tears, seep out in unexplainable depression, or ooze internally, resulting in undiagnosed illnesses. The one thing we can be sure of is this: repressed pain never leaves on its own.

People carry all manner of pain from disappointments, failures, betrayals, and losses. In our hectic world, the most efficient and acceptable way of dealing with emotional pain is to get so busy that we have no time to think about it. This alleviates our discomfort, so we carry on, seemingly no worse for wear. However, the avoidance of pain keeps us from going through the process of forgiveness. When we refuse to feel the full impact of the pain, we do not allow it to do its necessary work on our character.

Counterfeits of Forgiveness

Being convinced that we need to forgive is only the first lap of a long and arduous race; once we start moving toward the goal of forgiveness, we're going to be tempted to stop along the way at three counterfeit goal lines.

Counterfeit goal #1: Minimizing

For several months Sonny had been seeing his pastor, Raul, about chronic depression. Gradually the two of them were piecing together the fragments of Sonny's shattered childhood. Raul had known Sonny's family for years, and he was a patient and compassionate listener. But after several weeks of little or no progress, Raul finally confronted Sonny.

"Look, you keep going over the same story, repeating the same lame explanations, making the same excuses for your parents. I think we need to look at the whole picture a little more carefully. And when we do, you're going to have to see their abuse for what it was."

Sonny was immediately defensive. "Oh, come on. They may have knocked me around a little, but it wasn't really abuse. Abuse is where parents lock their kids in closets for weeks. Or starve them. Or beat them to death. My folks were a little rough, but that's all."

"Sonny, how often did your parents hit you? Once a month? Once a week?"

There was a long pause. Sonny's eyes scanned the ceiling. Finally he responded, "Oh, maybe a couple of times a day, but they—"

Raul interrupted, "Sonny, hitting you, slapping you, and whipping you two or three times a day is *not* what loving parents do. They were hateful, angry people who were addicted to alcohol. They were abusers. They didn't love you the way they should have. That's the reality. If you want to forgive them, do it. But forgive the worst they did; don't forgive a watered-down version. They were terrible parents. Period."

Sonny sat with his face in his hands. For years he had clung to the false belief that his parents had really loved him. During the next few minutes the sad truth began to settle in. In the following weeks and months, Sonny passed through the common stages of grief: denial, rage, bargaining, resignation, and eventual acceptance. Finally he forgave his parents, and when he did, he forgave them for the full measure of their violence and brutality.

Once Sonny faced the severity of his ordeal, he never again diminished it, dismissed it, or pretended it didn't matter. Having faced the truth about his parents, Sonny was able to grieve and forgive, and eventually his depression began to lift.

Counterfeit goal #2: Excusing

Peter Bliss, the adult ministry director at the city mission in Cleveland, Ohio, had been running debt-canceling forums for a number of months. He based much of what he was doing on the ideas in Dave's book *Forgiving Our Parents, Forgiving Ourselves,*[1] so he invited Dave to Cleveland to see what was happening.

Saturday morning, when Peter zeroed in on the need to begin the process of forgiveness with our parents, someone raised the objection, "But they did the best they could." Then, during a break, Dave listened as several of the men told stories about parents who did *not* do the best they could—they did that which was cruel and evil. Yet each man seemed obligated to say, "But they probably did their best."

Excusing bad behavior is a way of trying to fix the past

by rewriting it. When we give up this futile attempt, God can begin turning death into life, disappointment into joy, and misery into mission.

The men and women Dave met at the city mission in Cleveland were a testimony of this. At the end of the Saturday morning workshop, Peter asked members of the audience to write a letter of unconditional forgiveness to their parents. On Sunday morning, the participants came with their letters. One by one they moved to the front and read them. Then they walked to a table, picked up a lighted candle, and burned the letter, symbolically canceling the debt. They all had much further to go in the healing journey, but this was an important and memorable first step.

Counterfeit goal #3: Avoiding

Dave's father died when Dave was twenty-three. For years Dave expressed no grief concerning the hurt done to him by his father. Then he came across this statement:

> Genuine forgiveness does not deny anger but faces it head on. If I can feel outrage at the injustice I have suffered, can recognize my persecution as such, and can acknowledge and hate my persecutor for what he or she has done, only then will the way to forgiveness be open to me.[2]

By refusing to acknowledge anger at the offense, Dave was not forgiving it; he was simply avoiding it. Avoiding, like minimizing and excusing, is not forgiving. To forgive, we must forgive reality. Without an honest emotional response to the total, undiminished wrongs we suffer, we cannot genuinely forgive those wrongs or fully pardon those who inflicted them. If we don't fully acknowledge the hurt our parents or others have caused, we end up with a watered-down version of forgiveness.

Situations like these present a dilemma. The trend has been for adult children to blame all their emotional disturbances and character weaknesses on their inept or evil parents. As a result, some good parents have been falsely accused. In light of that overemphasis, careful counselors encourage people to take responsibility for themselves and not blame Mom and Dad for all their woes. This is good, except when people then move to the opposite extreme and conclude that because they can't blame their parents neither can they acknowledge that their parents did anything wrong. This is silliness.

When we encourage people not to blame parents, we are not saying they should not acknowledge the effects of what their parents did; we are saying they should not use their parents' bad behavior to excuse their own.

This is an important distinction. Placing blame is different from acknowledging effects. We can acknowledge that people behave badly without blaming them for our own bad behavior. It is essential that we all take responsibility for ourselves, as the previous chapter emphasized. However, it is also essential that we be honest as to what we are taking responsibility for. Part of what we take responsibility for is our response to all the things that happen to us, which includes our upbringing. We don't deny that bad things happen; we simply refuse to perpetuate the badness.

It is a sad fact that some people *were* raised by cruel, selfish parents who committed acts that can only be described as evil. Oddly, however, it is these people who often have a hard time accepting how bad Mom and Dad were. They are the ones likely to minimize or excuse the faults and abuse rather than see the reality of them.

Before any one of us can release the past and take responsibility for the future, we must be truthful about both. In other words, we must get to the place where we can say, "Terrible things happened to me, but I *refuse* to make anyone else suffer for it. I will not perpetuate evil in the world."

It is true that all of us were shaped by our upbringing; it is also true that all of us were raised by imperfect parents. Although some parents could be classified as evil, most were a mixture of good and bad, as my experience illustrates.

I grew up in a home that was centered on the church. My parents were devout Christians with a growing faith. The older I get, the more I appreciate their unwavering commitment to Jesus Christ. But there was a crack in their faith. They got caught up in trying to look good to other church members rather than in building an authentic family where truth had precedence over appearances.

As a result, a pernicious habit developed in our home. We all learned to lie. Just a little, of course. We distorted the truth just slightly to make things look better, easier, prettier, or healthier than they really were. And since we did this to make Christ's work in us appear more profound, it seemed OK. So all three sons grew up creating a reality for ourselves that did not exist. What a tough thing for me to face as a minister of truth: I was a liar. But I did face it, and I continue to work at seeing things honestly and presenting them truthfully. I do not blame my parents for the choice I made to lie. Nor do I excuse or rationalize my deceit because it was accepted practice in our family. But I do acknowledge that lying was a destructive habit I learned at home.

When reviewing the past, our focus must be truth, not blame. If your parents were abusive, distant, phony, mean, or destructive, accept it so you can forgive the reality and be free to move on. If they were loving, kind, supportive, and strong, accept that truth as well and forgive yourself for responding badly to the positive character they displayed.

Obstacles to Forgiveness

Pastor Walter Everett's twenty-three-year-old son was shot to death in cold blood. After the killer was behind bars, the pastor had a large, impossible task to perform. For months he struggled with the biblical command to forgive.

In a subsequent hearing, the murderer told the judge and those assembled in the courtroom that he was sorry, but his voice and manner seemed insincere to all who heard him. This made forgiveness even more difficult for the grieving pastor.

It is always difficult to give even an inch of grace to someone whose actions have forever changed the course of our lives. It is especially difficult when the person makes a mockery of sorrow, repentance, and remorse.

But Pastor Everett knew that forgiveness was not an option. Eventually, in an act that amounted to nothing short of sheer determination and stubborn obedience, he composed a letter of forgiveness to the killer.

The pastor later learned that the young man, after reading the letter, had fallen to his knees in contrition. Sobbing beside his prison bunk, the killer had asked Jesus to forgive his sins and come into his heart.

When Pastor Everett mailed his letter he had no idea what the result of his obedience would be. Neither do any of us. Pastor Everett had plenty of "good" reasons not to forgive his son's killer, but he knew that none of them were good enough.

Few people verbalize their excuses for refusing to forgive, but they generally fall into one of two categories: fear or misconception.

Fear

The reason many of us refuse to forgive is our fear of loss. And there's no denying that forgiveness requires us to give up attitudes and actions that are important to us.

Fear of losing the energy that anger produces

Some people are reluctant to let go of the burning energy that rage generates. It is like a fuel that keeps them moving. Without it they would likely descend into despair and purposelessness because their anger is their purpose.

Fear of losing leverage in the relationship

Those who are still smarting from pain are not eager to risk being hurt again. They assume that if they forgive the guilty party, he or she will feel free to repeat the offense. This brings up an important point: *Forgiveness does not guarantee change in the other person's behavior.* Forgiveness is an act of obedience, not a tool of manipulation. It is a way of cleaning up the grudges and resentments that damage us. Although we cannot stop people from hurting themselves, we can, in some situations (if we are not legally or morally tied to the offender), guard ourselves against repeated injury. By removing ourselves from the relationship or by changing the rules of engagement, we can limit the person's ability to continue hurtful behavior.

Fear of losing hope for a better relationship

Some people have expectations for friends and family that are too high. As years go by, repeated foolish choices and ongoing evidence of serious character flaws devastate those who expect too much. In such cases, it is necessary to forgive people simply for being who and what they are and to accept that they probably are not going to change.

Fear of losing power and control

Refusing to forgive keeps others in our debt. In families, we often see parents who hold some wrong against an adult child, exacting payment in visits, gifts, and favors. "I'll never let him forget!" is their sinister form of motivation, and it works—at least for a while. But the toll it takes in resentment and estrangement outweighs any secondary gains. Although forgiving *feels* like an act of surrender, those who've done it know it's an act requiring tremendous strength.

Fear of losing the image of superiority

Holding an offense against another person places us in a "good guy, bad guy" picture with ourselves wearing the white hat. Imagining that we are better than others makes us feel good, but such a prideful attitude is unacceptable to God. When we hold people captive to our judgment, we play God in their lives. This places us in an unwinnable wrestling match with our Creator, who, as the apostle James reminded us, "opposes the proud" (James 4:6). To forgive someone, we have to lower ourselves to their level—just as Jesus did for us—and acknowledge that we are soul mates in sin.

Misconceptions

Some of the greatest obstacles to forgiveness are the misconceptions about what it is. Realizing what forgiveness is *not* may make it easier.

It is not condoning the behavior

Once we understand that the act of forgiving does not compromise our moral standard by condoning the offense, we are in a position to forgive even the worst of sins. To forgive is not saying, "What you did is OK." It is saying, "The consequences of your behavior belong to God, not to me." When we forgive, we transfer the person from our own system of justice to God's. To forgive is to recognize that the wrong done against us is a debt of sin, and all sin is against God. Therefore, in forgiving, we transfer the debt from our ledger of accounts to God's, leaving all recompense in his hands.

It is not forgetting what happened

It would be foolish to erase from mind some of the wrongs done to us. If we were to do so, we would never learn from our experiences and would walk right back into the same or a similar situation, only to face the same disappointments. What *can* eventually be forgotten are the raw emotions associated with the event. When we forgive, the terrible memories and feelings gradually diminish.

It is not restoring trust in the person

Trust is earned. It is something we give to those who deserve it. To blindly trust someone who has hurt us is naive and irresponsible. If a person is a thief, it is foolish to give her a key to your house. If he is a pedophile, you would be derelict to hire him as a babysitter. We can forgive people for the wrong they've done without extending to them an open invitation to do it again. It is foolish to trust an untrustworthy person.

It is not agreeing to reconcile

Forgiveness is a necessary step toward reconciliation, but reconciliation is not necessarily the goal of forgiveness. In fact, there are some situations when reconciliation is *not* a good idea. Reconciliation requires forgiveness, but forgiveness can be done without reconciling. If the other person is unwilling to reconcile due to bitterness or denial, we can still forgive. It is silly, if not dangerous, to press for reconciliation when the other person is unrepentant, unchanging, or unwilling.

It is not doing the person a favor

In Judaism, forgiveness is not required unless repentance is demonstrated and pardon is sought. But Jesus raised the standard of forgiveness to a higher level. According to him, we are to forgive even those who remain unrepentant. Forgiveness benefits the giver at least as much as it does the receiver, so we extend it whether or not the person asks for it.

It is not easy

Forgiving is difficult enough when it involves a onetime transgression. It verges on the impossible when the offense is ongoing. Such circumstances require an *attitude* of forgiveness, not simply an *act* of forgiveness.

When Peter asked Jesus how often he should forgive, Jesus gave an unsettling answer:

> Peter came to him and asked, "Lord, how often should I forgive someone who sins against me? Seven times?"
>
> "No, not seven times," Jesus replied, "but seventy times seven!"
> Matthew 18:21-22

Think about the mathematics of this statement. Can you imagine forgiving anyone, even for a minor offense, 490 times? Imagine having a neighborhood kid ride his bike through your garden every day of the week for seventy weeks. (That's one year, four months, and two weeks!) Jesus is asking us to do something that is humanly impossible. And that's the point. In and of ourselves we don't have enough forgiveness to go around. But God does. So when our limited resources run out and we are unable to forgive, we can ask him to forgive others *through* us. In so doing, we take one more step of obedience and allow ourselves to become a conduit of God's endless grace.

Forgiving God

Some people say there are times when we need to forgive God. This implies that God does wrong, which is never true. However, we may find it hard to place faith in God once we have in mind that he has let us down. When we attribute human characteristics to God and expect him to act in specific ways, we set ourselves up for disappointment. God is always trustworthy, but we do not always know his mind, his reasons, or his ultimate intentions, so we are prone to misinterpreting his actions in our lives.

Our problem with trusting God stems from our willful determination about what is good and right, not from his untrustworthiness. One thing is certain: we can trust him infinitely more than we can trust ourselves. This being the case, we ought to trust God to run the world the way he created it to run and not plead with him to run it our way.

When Forgiving Seems Impossible

Corrie ten Boom, one of the twentieth century's great Christian spokespersons, lost her sister and father in the Nazi death camps during World War II, and she nearly lost her own life too.

Years after her release, Corrie began to speak publicly on the subject of forgiveness, pleading with Christians to forgive those who have harmed them. Then she unexpectedly encountered what seemed to her the impossibility of forgiveness. Her book *The Hiding Place* recounts it this way:

> It was at a church service in Munich that I saw him, the former S.S. man who had stood guard at the shower room door in the processing center at Ravensbruck. He was the first of our actual jailers that I had seen since that time. And suddenly it was all there—the roomful of mocking men, the heaps of clothing, Betsie's pain-blanched face.
>
> He came up to me as the church was emptying, beaming and bowing. "How grateful I am for your message, *Fraulein*," he said. "To think that, as you say, He has washed my sins away!"

His hand was thrust out to shake mine. And I, who had preached so often to the people in Bloemendaal the need to forgive, kept my hand at my side.

Even as the angry, vengeful thoughts boiled through me, I saw the sin of them. Jesus Christ had died for this man; was I going to ask for more? Lord Jesus, I prayed, forgive me and help me to forgive him.

I tried to smile; I struggled to raise my hand. I could not. I felt nothing, not the slightest spark of warmth or charity. And so again I breathed a silent prayer. Jesus, I cannot forgive him. Give me your forgiveness.

As I took his hand in mine the most incredible thing happened. From my shoulder along my arm and through my hand a current seemed to pass from me to him, while into my heart sprang a love for this stranger that almost overwhelmed me.

And so I discovered that it is not on our forgiveness any more than on our goodness that the world's healing hinges, but on His. When He tells us to love our enemies, He gives, along with the command, the love itself.[3]

Whenever forgiveness seems impossible, we can remember this: Jesus Christ lives in us, and he can do what we cannot. And so we cling to the promise, "With God all things are possible."

Joseph found this out. Stuck in a foreign prison for a crime he did not commit, Joseph had much to be angry about. He could have lamented his lost opportunities and blamed his brothers; instead he allowed God to work in and through him.

[Potiphar] took Joseph and threw him into the prison where the king's prisoners were held, and there he remained. But the LORD was with Joseph in the prison and showed him his faithful love. And the LORD made Joseph a favorite with the prison warden. Before long, the warden put Joseph in charge of all the other prisoners and over everything that happened in the prison. The warden had no more worries, because Joseph took care of everything. The LORD was with him and caused everything he did to succeed.   Genesis 39:20-23

Joseph's captors recognized the work of God in his life and wanted to take advantage of it. Joseph ended up being second in command in the land of Egypt. Then a famine forced his brothers to come searching for food to survive. Joseph had the power—and some would say the right—to crush them with a single command. But he didn't. Instead of repaying evil with evil, which is the human way of doing things, Joseph repaid evil with good, which is God's way of doing things.

"Please, come closer," he said to [his brothers]. So they came closer. And he said again, "I am Joseph, your brother, whom you sold into slavery in Egypt. But don't be upset, and don't be angry with yourselves for selling me to this place. It was God who sent me here ahead of you to preserve your lives. This famine that has ravaged the land for two years will last five more years, and there will be neither plowing nor harvesting. God has sent me ahead of you to keep you and your families alive and to preserve many survivors. So it was God who sent me here, not you! And he is the one who made me an adviser to Pharaoh—the manager of his entire palace and the governor of all Egypt."   Genesis 45:4-8

Joseph looked beyond the evil his brothers had done and saw the hand of God at work for good. His example shows the power of forgiveness to release us from resentment and free us to enjoy the good that God intends for each of us.

Notes

1. Dave Stoop, *Forgiving Our Parents, Forgiving Ourselves* (New York: Vine, 1992, 1997).

2. Alice Miller, *For Your Own Good* (New York: Farrar, Straus, and Giroux, 1983).

3. Corrie ten Boom with John and Elizabeth Sherrill, *The Hiding Place* (Lincoln, Va.: Chosen Books, 1971; New York: Bantam, 1974), 238.

START TODAY!

How to Grieve, Forgive, and Let Go

- Accept the pardon of the Cross for yourself and extend it to others
- Acknowledge the wrongs done against you without excusing them
- Release the moral debts you hold against those who have hurt you
- Release yourself from moral debt God has forgiven
- Make amends to others for your wrongdoing (but not if doing so would hurt another person)
- Let go of grudges you have held against God for what he has allowed
- Refuse to confuse forgiving with excusing
- Continue to release others from your debt by forgiving them
- Continue to receive God's forgiveness according to his promises

BIBLICAL EXAMPLE

Joseph forgiving his brothers for selling him as a slave

BIBLE VERSES

Matthew 6:14-15: "If you forgive those who sin against you, your heavenly Father will forgive you. But if you refuse to forgive others, your Father will not forgive your sins."

Chapter 6
Transform Your Life

All praise to God, the Father of our Lord Jesus Christ.
God is our merciful Father and the source of all comfort.
He comforts us in all our troubles
so that we can comfort others.
When they are troubled,
we will be able to give them
the same comfort God has given us.

2 Corinthians 1:3-4

God is not looking for magnificent specimens of humanity.
He's looking for deeply spiritual, genuinely humble,
honest-to-the-core servants who have integrity.

—Charles Swindoll

THE YOUNG Moabite widow stood at a crossroads. The man she loved had died and so had his brother and father. Their deaths left three grieving women alone in a land where the only socially acceptable role for adult women was that of wife. Naomi, the mother of the two dead sons, was a foreigner in Moab. She had moved there with her husband and sons many years earlier to escape a famine in Israel. The sons had found wives and settled down, intending to stay. But now that her husband and sons were dead, Naomi had no reason to stay. The famine had ended in Israel, so Naomi decided to return home to Bethlehem. Her daughters-in-law, Ruth and Orpah, began the long journey with her, but along the way Naomi stopped.

"Go back to your mother's home," she urged them. "You have shown me great kindness, but there is no reason for you to accompany me. Go home and find new husbands among your own people."

The two young women wept at the thought of separation, but eventually Orpah was convinced to turn around and go home. Ruth, however, refused.

"Don't ask me to leave you and turn back," she pleaded. "Wherever you go, I will go; wherever you live, I will live. Your people will be my people, and your God will be my God" (Ruth 1:16).

Ruth's choice was more than just a declaration of loyalty to her mother-in-law; it was a declaration of belief in the God of Israel. She was not simply leaving her family and homeland; she was rejecting their religion and gods.

So the two women traveled on alone—still sorrowful, still having nothing but their commitment to each other and to God, still feeling little hope for happiness.

Their arrival in Bethlehem created quite a stir. The women of the town exclaimed, "Can this be Naomi?"

Naomi's response revealed her hopelessness: "Don't call me Naomi," she told them. "Instead, call me Mara, for the Almighty has made life very bitter for me. I went away full, but the LORD has brought me home empty. Why call me Naomi when the LORD has caused me to suffer and the Almighty has sent such tragedy upon me?" (Ruth 1:20-21).

Naomi's judgment concerning God's work in her life was premature. She was looking at her immediate situation and making a conclusion about her entire life. She was judging the worth of her whole existence on one short period of time. Naomi was too distraught to see that God had more in mind for both her and Ruth than either could imagine. Had it not been for her daughter-in-law, Naomi would never have found out what it was.

Ruth, though new to the Jewish faith, had a stronger belief in Yahweh than did her mother-in-law, and she demonstrated it by making two crucial choices. She chose to believe God and to love her mother-in-law. Without love for Naomi, Ruth would have gone back to her own family. And without belief in the God of Israel, Ruth would have gone back to her family's gods. But she didn't. Her love for Naomi and her faith in God transformed the tragedy—not only for herself but also for her mother-in-law and for all future generations.

The powers of faith and love are still at work today, and they can still transform all of our circumstances and redeem even the most desperate life.

The Transforming Power of Faith

Whenever we struggle in a sinful habit we cannot break or get caught in some unpleasantness that has no end in sight, the idea of finding a purpose in it seems like nothing more than a pious platitude. We feel lucky if we can simply maintain the status quo. We can't imagine how such miserable circumstances could ever be transformed into something positive.

The reason many of us have trouble accepting the idea that God can transform pain into purpose stems from faulty thinking about God. We see him as a cosmic stage manager waiting in the wings to redesign the set whenever our circumstances become unpleasant. When we give the cue, we expect him to leap into action and change our surroundings in some mysterious way—apart from anything we do and regardless of whether or not *we* change. Then, when God does not change the setting on cue, we sigh in disgust and go about changing it for him.

But God is not an inept stage manager; he's the playwright, and he does not change the setting for the comfort and convenience of the characters. Throughout history God has been unfolding an intricate plot of redemption that transcends both the setting and the characters. To accomplish his plan, God needs cooperative characters who trust his direction and don't try to rewrite the script or change the stage directions.

God's plan involves certain principles that are nonnegotiable. They are not hidden, complicated, or difficult; and they are not mystical, magical, or even miraculous. They are simple truths that are common to all humans and essential for the health and well-being of society.

Although Ruth was relatively young in the Jewish faith, she had already internalized many of these truths, and when life took a turn for the worse, she acted upon them. In the wake of tragedy, Ruth exercised qualities that transformed her circumstances.

Kindness

In times of adversity, the natural response is to make ourselves the center of the universe. We focus all our attention and energy on trying to solve our problems and to relieve ourselves of the pain they're causing. But Ruth did not succumb to this temptation. Despite her own grief, she deferred to the needs of her mother-in-law.

The Jewish system of government allowed poor people to work as gleaners in the harvest fields. Landowners and the harvesters they hired were told to leave some grain in the fields for those who came along behind to glean. Shortly after arriving in Bethlehem, Ruth asked Naomi for permission to go pick up some of this leftover grain in the fields.

Ruth did not assert her right to work, but she obviously

did not expect to be taken care of by her mother-in-law. Even though Ruth was a guest in her mother-in-law's homeland, and even though she was equally grief stricken, she took upon herself the responsibility for the care of their fragile family, and in a kind, nondemeaning way she assured Naomi that she need not worry about their well-being.

Whenever we make tragedy our focal point, self-pity becomes our theme. We then become rude, impatient, and sarcastic, subconsciously thinking that if we make someone else feel bad, we'll feel better. But we don't; we feel worse instead. Ruth didn't fall into this trap. She made someone else's needs her focal point and remained kind and respectful.

Industriousness
Even though Ruth was still in mourning over the death of her husband, she did not use her adversity as an excuse for laziness. She was willing to work even though she was unfamiliar—and probably uncomfortable—with the people and their customs. The regular workers noticed her dedication to the task and mentioned it to the landowner, Boaz, saying to him, "She asked me this morning if she could gather grain behind the harvesters. She has been hard at work ever since, except for a few minutes' rest in the shelter" (Ruth 2:7). Work is often the last thing we feel like doing in times of crisis, but it's often the best thing for us.

Humility
When Boaz showed Ruth kindness, she bowed before him and exclaimed, "What have I done to deserve such kindness? I am only a foreigner" (2:10). Ruth did not expect special treatment from Boaz to make up for the difficult circumstances of her life, and she expressed surprise that he considered her actions exceptional.

Gratitude

After Boaz complimented Ruth for the care she was giving her mother-in-law, Ruth responded graciously, saying, "You have comforted me by speaking so kindly to me, even though I am not one of your workers" (2:13). Although Ruth probably was accustomed to a higher standard of living in Moab, she was grateful to be treated as well as a lowly servant girl in this foreign land.

This is by no means an exhaustive list of the qualities capable of transforming circumstances, but it's enough to show the category they all fall into. The qualities we need to transform our circumstances are those that elevate other people above ourselves and our problems. Ruth put Naomi's needs above her own, and she used her misfortune as an opportunity to minister to her mother-in-law, not as an excuse to hurt others or to get something from them.

Transforming Tragedy

At age five, Carol saw her alcoholic father sexually molest her babysitter. Sometime later, her mother divorced him and married another abusive alcoholic. Carol's stepfather's lewd comments made her feel as if she were a body without a soul. The one thing she thanked God for was a dead-bolt lock on her bedroom door, the only room in the house that had one, and she used it often.

Not surprisingly, Carol grew up and married an abusive alcoholic. The scarred grooves of her soul were a perfect match for his abusive patterns. It was not long before his verbal tirades escalated to physical abuse. To Carol, the bloodstains on her clothes were like a big red blot covering her entire life, excluding her from all hope of finding fulfillment and purpose.

While still in her twenties, Carol divorced her husband,

but she could not divorce herself from the residue of abuse, bad choices, and faulty thinking that comprised her life. After the divorce, despair hovered over her like a cloud, darkening her life and blocking her vision of God.

Then a coworker told Carol how Jesus Christ had changed her life. The coworker invited her to attend a recovery group with others who had been through similar trauma.

Carol accepted the invitation, even though she expected to find angry, depressed people obsessing over the past. But instead she found people with smiling faces, encouraging words, and peace in their hearts. She was drawn to them and to the Savior who had transformed their lives. She accepted their Savior as her own and felt him lift the burden of her past. The transformation the others had experienced began for her as well.

Before long she was able to forgive her ex-husband and others who had hurt her. She became active in church and was baptized. She started to study the Bible and learned how to minister to others. Now she is a lay pastor and assists with the church's support groups for sexually abused women. She also has married a loving man very different from her previous husband and the other men who damaged her life.

Carol is radiant when she tells how Christ changed her life. She is transforming her pain into purpose by using it to point people to new life in Jesus.

Once we have overcome any problem or survived any tragedy, the loving response is to help others do the same. In other words, we transform our circumstances by finding a way to use them for good. Whenever God heals one person, he plants a seed of healing. Each person who is healed can then multiply the healing by extending it to others, thereby becoming an agent of God's transforming power.

Transforming Failure

Judy was a defiant, determined, adolescent girl; Jerry was a rebellious, risk-taking, teenage boy. His idea of fun was to taunt the local small-town police into chasing him. Their battered and beat-up Chevrolets were no match for his souped-up Pontiac, so he would play cat and mouse with them for a while and then speed away, leaving them chasing each other through clouds of dust. When the thrill of the chase wore off, Jerry flirted with more serious crime and eventually wound up in jail for burglary.

Judy's idea of fun was to flirt with Jerry, the guy with the worst reputation in town. She made it her goal to get a date with him, and she succeeded. Soon they were the hottest couple in Hudsonville. "For the first time in my life I felt I was somebody," Judy says. "I was Jerry Schreur's girlfriend."[1]

Judy continued to be "somebody," but not the somebody her widowed mother hoped she would be. When Judy's mother quoted Scripture to her daughter about not being "unequally yoked" with unbelievers, Judy envisioned ripping the pages out of the Bible and cramming them down her mother's throat.

Three years later, Judy's dream and her mother's worst fears came true. Judy was pregnant. She and Jerry would have to get married. Abortion was not an option, and illegitimate babies were not yet socially acceptable. So they did what they had to do. Not a good formula for living happily ever after.

Working against the forces of evil, anger, and rebellion in their lives, however, was one force for good, a Christian man named Perc, who befriended Jerry. Where everyone else saw hopelessness, Perc saw an opportunity to dispense grace. While other Christians moved away from the young couple, Perc and his wife moved toward them. And that made all the difference.

Perc invited Jerry to use his garage as a place to repair his motorcycle engine. While the two worked side by side getting the bike to work, Perc patiently showed Jerry how to make his life work. He didn't scold Jerry for his rebellious-ness, and he didn't preach about where he was going to end up if he didn't turn his life around. In fact, he didn't even use many words. He simply showed Jerry a better way to live.

And Jerry believed. First he believed Perc, and then he believed God. Jerry's conversion and consequent change reignited Judy's faith. She reconfirmed the decision to follow Jesus she had made as a young girl.

Jerry began reading and studying the Bible and decided he wanted more formal Bible training, but he had a big obstacle to overcome: no high school diploma. Jerry refused to take no for an answer, however. His recalcitrance, which once made him a terror in his small town, had been trans-formed into persistence, which helped him find a way into college. He submitted an application to a local Bible college and managed to get in. After earning his degree, Jerry taught at the school for a while and eventually became the minister of congregational care at a large midwestern church. He now spends much of his time counseling couples preparing for marriage as well as those contemplating divorce.

Jerry and Judy have devoted their lives to helping cou-ples avoid making the mistakes they made—or recover from making them. Judy is a popular speaker at women's retreats and seminars, and the two often pair up to do marriage con-ferences and retreats. They also have written several books, the most recent of which tells much of their story and was written with their oldest son, Jack, the product of their rebelliousness.[2] The same year the book was published, Jerry the high school dropout became Jerry Schreur, Ph.D., as Michigan State University granted him a doctorate.

Jerry and Judy could have kept their sin a secret. It was, in fact, the expected thing to do in their religiously conservative community. Even today, some people wonder why they continue to tell the story, believing that others will think badly of them if they find out the truth.

But Jerry and Judy have learned the freedom that comes from telling the truth—both for themselves and for the many others they encounter who are unable to transcend their circumstances because they are bound in sin and secrecy.

Part of redeeming the past involves testifying to what God has done and is doing in our lives. This kind of self-revelation epitomizes true love. Doing so, however, runs counter to modern culture. As Jerry and Judy's story illustrates, it also runs counter to the religious culture of churches in which people claim to believe in the theological concept of total depravity but for some reason want to create the illusion that they are exempt.

Once we've been transformed by God's love, we will be compelled to act as his agents of love and grace in the lives of others. If we have experienced hope after tragedy or found meaning in the wake of purposelessness, it is selfish to not tell others what we have found. When God's love is at work in our lives, it will drive us toward fellow strugglers to whom we will humbly admit our wanderings from God and proclaim his mercy and grace in drawing us back to himself.

Jerry and Judy found spiritual healing, and they can't imagine keeping the cure a secret even though it has meant exposing their sin.

Suppose you are a research scientist who has a hunch as to how to cure the AIDS virus. You set up your laboratory, design your experiments, and test your hypothesis. The initial results show promise, so you do further testing. These results are positive as well, so you take the next step. Eventually you are convinced that your findings are correct and that your treatment is effective. But then you begin having second thoughts. What if there is a flaw in your research and you lose credibility with your peers? What if there are serious side effects to the treatment and you are sued? What if someone steals credit for the cure and you receive no monetary reward? These questions make you fearful, so you decide to sit on your findings. As a result, thousands of people continue to suffer and die needlessly.

What kind of person would keep this knowledge from the world? Is it too strong to call such a person evil? I think not. Only the forces of darkness would want healing information kept secret; God's love would compel you to proclaim your discovery.

Now suppose that you are not a doctor and that you have no scientific background. If you were to announce to the world that you had a cure for AIDS, imagine the reaction. Disbelief. Rejection. Ridicule. Isolation. People would think you were a nut. But even so, would that be justification for keeping the cure to yourself? Of course not.

But here's where the illustration hits close to home. There are millions of people in this world who are wasting away spiritually. Not everyone has a friend with AIDS, but we all have at least one friend who is living without the transforming presence of Jesus Christ in his or her life. Some of us may not know a single person with AIDS, but we all are surrounded by people who have a terminal spiritual disease.

Staring from the cover of *Muscle & Fitness* magazine was the smiling face of male model Gunter Schlierkamp. Though seated in an apparently relaxed position, his hulking muscles and protruding veins looked anything but relaxed. Inside the magazine, more photos of men with bulging biceps popped from the pages. This was, after all, the issue that covered Joe Weider's Mr. and Masters Olympia contest.

What do all these men do with such massive muscles? Become soldiers and defend our nation? Become police officers and fight crime in our cities? Become bodyguards and protect widows and orphans from assault? No. They pose for judges, compete against one another, and admire themselves.

It is easy to recognize the futility of this kind of strength in a bodybuilding magazine, but we've got much the same thing happening in churches.

Some Christians are like spiritual bodybuilders. They read about spirituality, feed themselves a steady diet of healthy thoughts, and go to church as faithfully as bodybuilders go to the gymnasium. As a result of their efforts they become spiritually strong, but they never use their spiritual strength to help people—only to get other spiritual bodybuilders to admire them.

These people do manage to solve their problems and improve their circumstances. But because their motives are selfish, the change never benefits anyone but themselves. If they have a problem and work it out, they simply go on with life, keeping what they have learned to themselves, showing no concern that someone else might benefit from it.

People who are being spiritually renewed and not just physically comforted feel compelled to tell others about the transformation in their lives so others can experience it as well. None of us can go back and undo the bad that has happened, but we all can find ways to use the bad to achieve something good. That is what John is doing.

While driving under the influence of alcohol, John crossed the center line of the highway and collided head-on with a man riding a motorcycle, killing him instantly and

robbing the man's family of a husband, father, and grandfather. The family of the dead man was devastated, and so
was John. Everyone involved wanted to turn back the clock
and make the terrible reality *un*happen. But they couldn't.
What they could do, however, was transform the tragedy
into something positive—something that would help prevent
similar tragedies.

John and the dead man's daughter teamed up to tell their
story to those who might be inclined to drink and drive. It
was not easy for the daughter to tell what she and her family
lost when her dad's life was snatched from them. It was not
easy for John to admit that he was the cause of all their pain.
Yet both continue to do so. They are turning their pain into
purpose, their misery into a mission. In so doing, they are
making something positive out of something tragic, a choice
that always accomplishes the purposes of God.

Perhaps you consider yourself too shy to do anything
like this. Or maybe you don't like being "pushy" about
your faith. There are many excuses for not telling others
what God has done for us, but no good reasons. All of us
can learn to tell others the tragic circumstances of our
lives—whether it is something terrible that happened to us
or something terrible that we did—and then tell how God's
power has transformed our situations and ourselves.

When God's love changes us, it then flows *through* us to
others. When we experience God's comfort in the midst of
a painful ordeal, we want to extend that comfort to others
in similar circumstances.

The key is to look at each situation with eyes of faith
and to ask God for help in transforming our circumstances,
rather than pleading with him to remove us from them. This
gives him the freedom he needs to do the necessary work
and to make the necessary change in our hearts, not just in
our circumstances.

In the film *The Shawshank Redemption,* a banker serving a life sentence for a murder he did not commit redeems his time by using it for good. He uses his financial skills to help the guards, he teaches uneducated prisoners to read, and he helps build a prison library.

Wherever we are, whatever our situation, we can transform it by using it as an opportunity to help others. To do this, we need only look at the people around us, identify their needs, and do whatever we can to help them.

Stories of transformation often are highlighted by happy endings. A sin is confessed. A broken marriage is restored. An addiction is broken. A ministry is begun. These encouraging reports can strengthen the faith of believers and cause others to trust God.

That is exactly what happened after Peter's failure. At their last meal together, Jesus told Peter, "I have pleaded in prayer for you, Simon, that your faith should not fail. So when you have repented and turned to me again, strengthen your brothers" (Luke 22:32).

Jesus' prayer for Peter was answered in a dramatic way. On the day of Pentecost, when the Holy Spirit came on the believers with tremendous power, who jumped up to preach the sermon? Peter. Who challenged the religious leaders who had arrested Jesus? Peter. Who preached with boldness even though he was arrested, beaten, and threatened? Bold, passionate, impetuous Peter.

God didn't waste Peter's failure; he used it as a testimony of God's transforming power. Impulsive Peter became known as "the rock." This truth gives hope to every generation. All who have tried and failed to follow Jesus can look at the outcome of Peter's life and be encouraged. God doesn't erase our history; he uses it as the "before" picture to show the contrast between what we were like *without* him and what we are like *with* him. God is not a destroyer;

he is a redeemer. He doesn't get rid of the characteristics that make us unique; he redeems them for his use.

But not every story has a happy ending—at least not yet. Transformation is a process, not an event. Small achievements add up to great victories. Ruth had no guarantee that she would ever have another husband; she simply did what she believed was right and left the consequences in God's hands. She was faithful in a small thing (see Matthew 25:23)—in grief she remained kind, humble, and grateful—and God made her part of something very important: the ancestral line of his Son, the Messiah.

Even when we're in the midst of a struggle, we can encourage others if we're experiencing spiritual renewal. In fact, the coexistence of faith and pain in Ruth's life is as much of an encouragement as is the eventual happily-ever-after ending of her story.

Suppose that one of your children has locked you into a joyless struggle with his rebellion. Day in and day out you struggle to endure all that goes with it—the lies, the fear, the disappointment. Maybe someday things will change, but you can't imagine how. The hope of finding anything of value in this ugly situation eludes you. And yet, countless lives have been changed when parents in similar situations have turned their focus on the Lord and found a way to minister to others out of their own brokenness. It goes back to the story of the oyster from chapter 4—you may not be able to rid yourself of your own problem, but you can use it to make something of value for someone else.

In short, even when there is no happy ending to report—at least not yet—we still have the opportunity to transform our difficulties into something useful.

The very process of spiritual renewal and transformation promises something far better than escape. It promises change—change of heart. And that is the essence of redemption. Every limitation is a chance for God to do for us what we cannot do for ourselves. If we long to find purpose in our pain and desire to see good arise from the bad that has happened, God will show us how to transform our circumstances and he will redeem our lives.

The Redeeming Power of Love

Faith in God's transforming power is intertwined with hope in his redeeming love. People have a hard time imagining love that is unaffected by actions or attitudes. Human love is so fickle that using the term *unconditional* to describe love seems like an oxymoron. But it's not. God's love for us is beyond human understanding; our minds simply cannot grasp it.

People who have not yet come to terms with their own sinfulness are even more amazed at God's love for others than at his love for them. The idea that he could love the people we consider enemies is incomprehensible. Yet this is just another example of how far God's love extends. Even our enemies are beloved by him.

When we place our hope in a divine love of such magnitude, we finally see that whatever sin we have committed, whatever evil has been done to us, or whatever good thing life has taken from us can be used by God for good.

None of us can redeem our own lives. Redemption is not "pulling ourselves up by our own spiritual bootstraps." God is the Redeemer, with a capital *R*. And he is ready, willing, and able to do the necessary work of redemption. The only thing he requires is our willing cooperation.

Redeemed hearts: a new attitude

The life of the apostle Paul shows us what a new attitude looks like. He went from a prison to royal courts, from being a crowd pleaser to a martyr. He said, "I know how to live on almost nothing or with everything. I have learned the secret of living in every situation, whether it is with a full stomach or empty, with plenty or little. For I can do everything through Christ, who gives me strength" (Philippians 4:12-13).

Contentment and gratitude do not come naturally, especially when we are in emotional or physical pain. They intrude on self-pity and melancholy. But they are choices we can make. And they are the choices God wants us to make because they reflect a humble spirit of worship and praise, which will lift us above and beyond our problems.

Redeemed minds: a new reality

Pride often seduces us into rigid adherence to our own idea of perfection, which we rationalize or spiritualize as personal piety. However, when we pass through suffering and allow God to redeem us, we begin to see life as it really is. Even though we are made in God's image, each of us is a flawed human being. Through redemption, however, we are no longer slaves to degrading sinfulness or prideful self-righteousness. Instead, we become God's agents of grace in the world. We willingly get our hands dirty because we know that it is in the mud and mire that we find those who need us most.

Redeemed perspective: a new view of adversity

Some of the greatest benefits we gain from our troubles are the lessons we learn. We learn, for example, that failure is an event, not a character description, and that the only real failure is giving up.

In a similar sense, problems can be our greatest opportunities. While it does no good to ask *why* this has happened, asking *how* I can transform this difficulty into something good begins the process of transformation and redemption. Every problem comes with an opportunity wrapped inside it, and the efforts we make to unwrap the problem and get to the opportunity become ways of helping others do the same.

Problems also introduce us to new friends and bring change to mundane schedules. They teach us exciting new truths. They lead us down unexplored paths. Problems allow us to exercise unused skills. They give us something to offer others. Most important of all, problems put us in touch with God. For it is in times of trouble that we learn to appropriate the strength of God.

One of the great mysteries of God is his ability to take the tragic things that happen and turn them into something good. He redeems the past—all of it.

The gospel that saves souls also salvages circumstances. God's Word asserts, "And we know that God causes everything to work together for the good of those who love God and are called according to his purpose for them. For God knew his people in advance, and he chose them to become like his Son, so that his Son would be the firstborn among many brothers and sisters" (Romans 8:28-29).

God has a purpose for everyone who loves him. That purpose is unique for each individual, but it has one common characteristic: everyone is being conformed to the image of Jesus Christ. No matter what we go through, God can use that experience to make us Christlike.

God uses troubles to provide us with a new view of his sovereign rule over humanity. For this to happen, we have to abandon some preconceived religious ideas like the old lie that good things happen to good people and bad things are punishment for bad behavior. This Christianized karma is a perversion of truth. So is the false hope that God will always keep us from pain. No one who follows a crucified

Christ—the One who says, "Take up your cross and follow me"—can hope to avoid pain.

When our lives are being spiritually renewed, our desires and priorities change. Instead of hiding our sinfulness and avoiding personal pain, we reveal our sinfulness so we can use it to relieve the pain of others.

Turning Misery into Mission

The triumph of Christ's resurrection is the template for all redeemed lives. When Jesus overcame death, he defeated the worst enemy of all. Today we are left to battle with far lesser foes, knowing that he has already won the war. We are simply gaining inner strength through hope and proving our faith by showing others how to claim the victory God has already won.

People today are striving for personal potential, self-empowerment, and inner strength. Christianity has a completely opposite way of thinking; it is a faith full of paradoxes. We die to live, we lose to find, and we become weak to gain strength.

As mortals we have little comprehension of eternity, and seldom do we use the eternal values just mentioned to guide our lives. Instead, we look at our immediate needs and formulate a plan for God to follow in meeting them. Then we hold on to that plan as if it were a religious conviction. This kind of thinking keeps us focused on getting our own way rather than on releasing God's redemptive power in our lives.

When we stop trying to control the outcome of every situation and stop demanding that God resolve our problems according to our dictates, we unlock the door for God to show us his redemptive purpose. Praying, "Your will be done . . ." gets us out of God's way and removes any of our small-minded ideas as to how things are supposed to work out.

Victory comes when we have more faith in God's power than in our own and more desire to see God's plan unfold than our own.

Hope: find a healing environment

A healing environment is one where people love God, understand our circumstances, and know how to show compassion while not allowing us to wallow in self-pity. Such a place allows us to grieve our losses and express our feelings without fear of rejection or criticism but at the same time keeps us moving forward lest we become comfortable in our misery.

By becoming part of a group—either a formal support group or an informal group of friends—that encourages and upholds people with struggles like ours, we can put our pain to work by processing it openly and honestly. When others hear what we are going through, they find hope in our small victories and encouragement in our perseverance, and vice versa.

Faith: find a way to help others

Finding a way to help others is an expression of faith. It shows that we believe in the sovereignty of God. We don't have to wait until the pain is gone for transformation to begin. However, we must be convinced that God has allowed the pain for a reason and that he wants to use it for good. This conviction helps us to let go of any grudge we are holding against God for what he has allowed in our lives.

Finding a way to help others requires that we ask two questions: "What is God doing?" and "How can I get into the flow of his activity?" When we ask these questions, ideas will come. And once we begin doing this, the *why* question, which once seemed so important, becomes irrelevant. The best answer to *why?* is always *what?* When we stop asking "Why has God allowed this?" and begin asking "What does he want me to do with it?" we are ready for God to start his work in us.

Ongoing prayer for wisdom and faithful study of his Word are essential for gaining insight and a truthful understanding of our circumstances. When we see the truth about God and about ourselves and our circumstances, we also see that God is at work in the world and that his work in us is not yet complete. Great hope is found in the powerful words Paul wrote to the Ephesian believers: "Now all glory to God, who is able, through his mighty power at work within us, to accomplish infinitely more than we might ask or think" (Ephesians 3:20).

That is certainly what God did for Naomi. Though lacking in faith herself, she was the beneficiary of her daughter-in-law's faith. Naomi believed that God had treated her badly by taking her husband and sons from her. She focused on what God had taken away and failed to see what he had given—a daughter-in-law who was better than seven sons. This attitude of ingratitude kept her from seeing the good God intended to do.

That was not true of Ruth, however. In times of trouble or tragedy, the natural response is to return to a place of comfort and familiarity. That's what Orpah did when she returned home. But Ruth chose the *un*familiar. She chose the way of faith.

Although Ruth transformed her circumstances by choosing faith over familiarity, she could not redeem herself. Someone else had to do that for her. She could, however, place herself in a situation where redemption was possible. And that's what she did.

Jewish law allowed the nearest male relative to marry a widowed woman and become her "family redeemer." Boaz was a well-respected and wealthy man in the community, and he was also a relative of Naomi's husband. When Boaz saw Ruth picking up leftover grain in his field, as poor people were allowed to do, he noticed her qualities and took a special interest in her.

Boaz fell in love with Ruth and joyously fulfilled the role of "redeemer." He married the young widow, and they became the parents of Obed, who became the grandfather of Israel's great King David.

This made Naomi a grandmother, and the women to whom she had once grumbled about God's unfair treatment now said to her:

> "Praise the LORD, who has now provided a redeemer for your family! May this child be famous in Israel. May he restore your youth and care for you in your old age. For he is the son of your daughter-in-law who loves you and has been better to you than seven sons!"
>
> Naomi took the baby and cuddled him to her breast. And she cared for him as if he were her own. The neighbor women said, "Now at last Naomi has a son again!" And they named him Obed. He became the father of Jesse and the grandfather of David. Ruth 4:14-17

Ruth became one of the heroines of the Jews, lauded to this day, and she is one of only five women mentioned by name in the genealogy of Jesus Christ (see Matthew 1). Ruth transformed her circumstances and allowed God to redeem her life. She turned her pain into purpose and her misery into a mission by exercising faith in God and love for others.

Notes

1. Jerry and Judy Schreur, *When Prince Charming Falls Off His Horse* (Colorado Springs: Victor, 1997), 17.
2. Ibid.

START TODAY!

How to Transform Your Life

- Use what you have been through as a way of helping others
- Look for God's purpose in allowing whatever life brings
- Cooperate with God as he makes all things to work together for good
- Stop asking why and begin asking what—What does God want me to do?
- Allow humbling experiences to give you a servant's heart
- Choose not to wallow in self-pity
- Invest your life in the lives of others
- Look for ways to use your story and experience to help others
- Take your pain and turn it into purpose
- Take your misery and turn it into ministry

BIBLICAL EXAMPLE

Ruth receiving a new life in the company of God's people

BIBLE VERSES

2 Corinthians 1:3-4: "All praise to God, the Father of our Lord Jesus Christ. God is our merciful Father and the source of all comfort. He comforts us in all our troubles so that we can comfort others. When they are troubled, we will be able to give them the same comfort God has given us."

Chapter 7
Preserve Spiritual Gains!

Do not throw away this confident trust in the Lord.
Remember the great reward it brings you!
Patient endurance is what you need now,
so that you will continue to do God's will.
Then you will receive all that he has promised.

Hebrews 10:35-36

MOSES grew up with all the comforts and advantages that wealth and privilege provide. While his Hebrew relatives slaved under the hot desert sun to make bricks for their Egyptian captors, Moses enjoyed a life of leisure. Raised by Pharaoh's daughter in the luxury of the palace, Moses was schooled in all the wisdom of the Egyptians (see Acts 7:20-22).

Moses seemed to know, however, that his unusual circumstances were ordained by God for a higher purpose than Moses' personal comfort. That he was even alive was evidence of God's protection in his life. Every other male his age had been killed at birth in an attempt by Pharaoh to control the population of the Hebrew slaves. Pharaoh's solution was to murder all male children. But Moses' mother refused to cooperate with Pharaoh's evil plan; she came up with a plan of her own. She made a basket out of reeds, waterproofed it with pitch, placed her infant son inside, and launched the crude vessel into the Nile River toward the spot where Pharaoh's daughters did their bathing.

Unlike Pharaoh's plan, hers worked perfectly. When one of the servants retrieved baby Moses from the river, his sister, Miriam, offered to find a Hebrew woman to nurse him. The princess agreed, and so it happened that Moses' own mother was able to raise her son until the time he was weaned, which, according to some rabbis, may have been as old as age four.

During that time with his mother, Moses learned his true identity. So when he went off to the palace to take his place as the son of a princess, he knew he was adopted and he probably knew the reason there were no other male children his age among the captive Hebrews. Pieces of information his mother had told him about life as a slave merged with what he learned and how he lived as a privileged member of Pharaoh's family. The result in Moses was an aroused sense of justice. He seemed to know that he had a mission to fulfill.

At age forty, Moses ventured away from the palace to visit his relatives. While watching them work, he saw an Egyptian beat up one of the Hebrew slaves. Enraged, Moses avenged the crime and killed (some say accidentally) the Egyptian. Moses thought that surely his defense of the slave would tell the other captives that God intended to use him to rescue them. But they didn't see it that way. The next day Moses saw two slaves fighting, and he tried to make peace between them. But the one who was mistreating the other said, "Who made you a ruler and judge over us? Are you going to kill me as you killed that Egyptian yesterday?" (Acts 7:27-28).

Realizing for the first time that there had been a witness to his crime and that his life might be in danger, Moses fled to Midian. The man who once had a home in two places—among the Hebrew slaves and with Egyptian royalty—now was welcome in neither. His first attempts at fighting injustice had got him in so much trouble that he had to flee for his life.

But no sooner had he reached a safe distance from Egypt than another instance of injustice was set before him. This time a family of sisters was trying to water their father's sheep. Every time they got the flock near the well, a group of shepherds chased them away. Once again Moses intervened on behalf of the oppressed, and this time the results were better. The father of the young girls invited Moses to dinner and eventually gave him one of his daughters as a wife. Moses settled down in Midian with his new wife, had a family, and lived there quietly tending his father-in-law's sheep, apparently forgetting what he once had considered his mission in life.

As it turned out, however, Moses had been right about God's plan for using him. He'd only been wrong about God's timing. After Moses had been in Midian for forty years (making him the ripe old age of eighty), an angel appeared to him in the flames of a burning bush. Amazed at the sight, Moses went over to look more closely and heard the Lord's voice: "I am the God of your father—the God of Abraham, the God of Isaac, and the God of Jacob. . . . The cry of the people of Israel has reached me, and I have seen how harshly the Egyptians abuse them. Now go, for I am sending you to Pharaoh. You must lead my people Israel out of Egypt" (Exodus 3:6-10).

We would expect Moses to have jumped at the chance. After all, he had shown an interest in delivering his people from slavery forty years earlier. But when he was told to do it, Moses didn't jump; he didn't even budge. Instead he started to give reasons for *not* doing it. Now that God was ready, Moses wasn't. And now that God declared Moses to be ready, Moses insisted he wasn't.

At age forty, he had been well positioned to accomplish the task. As a member of Pharaoh's family, he had an in with the ruling powers. But by age eighty, he had lost his connections: "Who am I to appear before Pharaoh?" Moses demanded of God. "Who am I to lead the people of Israel out of Egypt?" (Exodus 3:11). At age forty, Moses had thought his people would realize that his unusual circumstances were planned by God to prepare him to deliver them from slavery. But by age eighty, he had lost the confidence of his calling: "What if they won't believe me or listen to me? What if they say, 'The LORD never appeared to you'?" he protested (4:1). Before, he had had the advantage of a good education. But after forty years his mental abilities were diminishing: "O Lord, I'm not very good with words" Moses argued (4:10). At age forty, Moses had acquired all the human qualifications needed for the task; by age eighty, he had lost them all.

When he was forty, Moses had had a relationship with Pharaoh that he could depend on; at eighty, he had to depend on his relationship with God. Before, Moses had had the best of human wisdom at his disposal; but now, he had to wait for God to dispense his wisdom. Forty years ago, Moses could have relied on his own strength and ability; now he had to rely on God's.

The change in Moses could be reduced to a simple statement: at age forty, Moses had seen the problem; but at age eighty, he saw God. And seeing God made all the difference. According to the writer of Hebrews, Moses kept going because he "kept his eyes on the one who is invisible" (Hebrews 11:27).

As it was for Moses, so it is for us: seeing God and keeping our eyes on him are what make the difference. To talk about preserving spiritual gains to anyone who has not had a personal encounter with God is at best a waste of time. Worse, it can result in mindless dependence on creeds or heartless adherence to ritual, both of which lead to spiritual death.

But a onetime encounter with God is not enough. One vision or victory is only the beginning. We must add to our experience daily by keeping our eyes always on the invisible God. That is how we protect ourselves from growing weary of God. You see, at age eighty, Moses still had a relationship with God. Sadly, we live in a day when many lose theirs by age forty.

But when we sense the presence of God, experience his work in our lives on a regular basis, and see his vision for the world, we *will* persevere. It is the vision of God's truth, beauty, and goodness that goes before us, leading us to pursue him and all that he declares "good."

The vision God has for the world is indeed good, but we cannot see it until God opens our eyes and reveals it to us. The fall of man, which the book of Genesis records so tersely, was not like falling off a stepladder; it was like falling off Mount Everest. We were not just dinged; we were demolished.

Once we realize that all of our desires were corrupted at the Fall, all of our thoughts were twisted, and all of our strength was diverted toward evil, we begin to realize how dangerous it is to rely on human strength, desire, or even wisdom.

Human strength fails when we see no results. Human motivation ends when applause and affirmation fade. And human wisdom tells us to get ahead and then quit. But God's strength becomes perfect when we are weak. His approval begins when we stop trying to please the crowd. And his wisdom says to stay behind (behind God, that is) and keep going.

In a letter to a young pastor the apostle Paul wrote, "Pay close attention to yourself and to your teaching; persevere in these things, for as you do this you will ensure salvation both for yourself and for those who hear you" (1 Timothy 4:16, NASB). According to this advice to Timothy, perseverance has two parts. First, we must pay attention to ourselves—to what we do and why we do it (not just to our motions but also to the motives behind them). Second, we must pay attention to our doctrine—to what we believe. Or, in terms the writer of James might use: we must persevere in faith and works—in truth *and* in obedience. When we pay close attention to our beliefs and behavior, we accomplish two things: we protect ourselves from falling into sin, and we preserve our spiritual gains.

Persevere in Truth

The pursuit of truth is not a popular pastime these days (unless, of course, we're pursuing truth about someone we want the goods on). The idea of absolute truth is even more unpopular, often eliciting smirks or sneers. The fundamental thinking of postmodern philosophy is that your truth may be all right for you, but my truth is all right for me. This thinking inevitably leads to the abandonment of a common moral standard, which then will lead to moral chaos.

Perhaps that's one of the reasons Jesus was so emphatic about truth. Matthew's Gospel quotes him thirty times as saying, "I tell you the truth." Jesus even called himself the truth: "I am the way, the truth, and the life," he told his disciples (John 14:6). In addition, Jesus prayed, "Sanctify them by the truth; your word is truth" (John 17:17, NIV).

Saturate our minds with truth

"Sin will keep you from this book, or this book will keep you from sin." This slogan has been written on the flyleaf of many Bibles given as gifts to young people entering their critical decision-making years. The purpose, of course, is to gently remind them of the importance of the Bible to their moral and spiritual health. Over the years, the slogan has become a cliche and has gradually lost its effectiveness. It has, however, never lost its truthfulness. And each generation, often through trial and error, proves it to be true.

In our generation we are watching the erosion of truth as a common cultural value. Philip Yancey, writing in *Books & Culture,* tells about a young man named Sam who decided to stop lying and find out what difference it would make in his life. "It helps people picture you and relate to you more reliably," Yancey quotes him as saying. "Truth can be positively beneficial in many ways."[1]

Sam learned that truth has a practical advantage, for which we can be thankful. But it is frightening to realize that there are many "Sams" who see no value in truth if it has no apparent or immediate practical and personal advantage.

It's too early to know for sure what the error of the following generation will be, but we're already beginning to catch hints of what their motto might be. As our criminal justice system strains under the weight of increased juvenile crime, we see clues in hardened young faces. Though few have yet put it into words, their message is becoming clear: "You can't stop me." And they will be right. For when amorality becomes the majority, or even an angry minority, society will be helpless to halt the deterioration. By then, truth will have lost its practical value, so the only motivation to remain truthful will be the belief that truth is good because God says it is so.

Sadly, each generation realizes its sins after it's too late to fix them. That is why, in coming years, we will need perseverance to protect our spiritual well-being. We will not, cannot, persevere in the spiritual life if our minds are permeated with anything other than God's truth. If for any reason we choose not to believe what God says is true, we will wander into confusion, stumble over doubt, and fall headlong into sin.

On the other hand, truth will keep us out of trouble because it guides us around every potential danger. What Jesus said to the people who believed him applies to us as well: "You are truly my disciples if you remain faithful to my teachings. And you will know the truth, and the truth will set you free" (John 8:31-32).

Truth is revealed in God's Word and, in Bible times, was communicated primarily through teaching and preaching. Average people, having no access to the Scriptures, could not study God's Word for themselves. They were dependent on spiritual leaders to feed them. Today we have a profusion of Bible translations, study Bibles, commentaries, and other references to supplement the teaching and preaching we hear at church. But a market saturated with religious books is not the same as minds saturated with truth. And the abundance of resources sitting on bookshelves does not guarantee godly lives.

To protect ourselves from the enemy, we must continually seek to learn the truth—the truth about God, about ourselves, and about God's purpose for our existence. And despite the advances of modern technology, the only ways to find it are still through prayer, Bible study, and fellowship with believers.

Some years ago I met a man who was trying to recover from an addiction to cocaine. I say "trying" because he did not grasp what was needed for recovery. Rather than work out the deeper problems that led him into addiction, he did the superficial thing that many do: he became religious. He started going to church and giving big chunks of money to Christian organizations. He even demanded that one group put the name of Jesus in their statement of purpose. The name of God would not do; he was adamant that they add the name of Jesus.

Ironically, just a couple of years later this man no longer believed that Jesus was the only means of salvation. He no longer even considered himself a Christian. He had become a universalist. To many it seemed like a 180-degree turn. But not really. After using religion to conquer his addiction, he had done nothing to grow spiritually. He had not taken the time to get to know Jesus. Although he had changed his behavior, his heart had not changed. For him, getting religion was like changing shirts. He had taken off the shirt of addiction and put on the one of religion. Religion is always external, whereas Christianity is internal; religion is always impersonal, whereas Christianity is personal. Christianity, in fact, rests on the belief that humans can have a personal relationship with the God of the universe.

The truth about God: protection against doubt

Since Creation, God has been making himself known to us; and since the Fall, we have been hiding ourselves from him. God has done cartwheels (figuratively speaking, of course) to convince us that he is merciful, faithful, mighty, awesome, impartial, gracious and compassionate, our refuge and strength, an ever-present help, good, holy, sovereign, forgiving, truthful, just, light, and love—to name just a few. When we allow these truths to permeate our minds, they change our desires and ultimately our behavior.

God sees all of eternity in a single glance. He's been intimately involved in every twist and turn of history. We can trust God to never make mistakes, and we can know that our trust is not misplaced. No matter how difficult our circumstances, his Word reminds us that what is impossible for us is possible with God (see Mark 10:27). When we begin seeing what God is working to accomplish in the world, we get excited about being on his side. We are no longer bound by our fears and limitations; we are eager to see the power of God unleashed in our lives.

The truth about ourselves: protection against pride

Humans are born to trouble, the Bible says of us, and who can argue? When we're not in trouble of our own making, we're surrounded by the troubles of others. There's simply no escaping it. But an amazing thing about the Bible is that it is able to show us how bad we are *without* making us feel bad about ourselves. Contrary to many unfair accusations, the Bible doesn't denigrate us by revealing what despicable creatures we are; it elevates us by showing us what glorious beings we can become. We have nothing to lose and everything to gain by acknowledging the awful truth about ourselves.

Surrender our desires to truth

Desire is a natural and healthy part of human existence, but like everything else, our desires have been corrupted by sin. Desires that are normal and natural have caused families to break up and civilizations to fall when people tried to satisfy them outside of God's prescribed plan. In fact, if we fail to surrender our desires to God's truth, destruction of some kind is inevitable; only the magnitude of it remains in question.

On the other hand, the surrender of our desires to God will keep us from developing destructive patterns of thought and, thus, behavior. One particularly destructive kind of thinking starts with the words *if only.* "If only I had . . . a better spouse, a better church, a better job, a better family, more money . . ."

When we allow ourselves to become dissatisfied, we are marching headlong into one of Satan's traps. If we are always looking for something more than God has given, we are destined to get what God says is not good for us to have.

- When we are dissatisfied with our spouse, our desire for intimacy may cause us to use someone other than our spouse as the way to satisfaction.
- When we are dissatisfied with our home, our desire for a more comfortable place to raise our families and entertain our friends may lure us into taking on unmanageable debt.
- When we are discontented with our children, our desire to have them be kind and well behaved may tempt us to become critical and harsh.

Satisfaction, on the other hand, has many spiritual benefits:

- It eliminates lustful thinking, which is the doorway to many sins.
- It eliminates anxiety, which lures us toward unhealthy forms of relief.
- It eliminates perfectionism, which results in destructive criticism.

Being satisfied is a sign of spiritual health, for it is evidence that we believe what Jesus taught in his most famous sermon:

> And why worry about your clothing? Look at the lilies of the field and how they grow. They don't work or make their

clothing, yet Solomon in all his glory was not dressed as beautifully as they are. And if God cares so wonderfully for wildflowers that are here today and thrown into the fire tomorrow, he will certainly care for you. Why do you have so little faith?

Matthew 6:28-30

God alone knows what we need and when we need it. And he is never late. As we learn to trust that he is in control, we will gladly surrender our desires to him and wait for him to act on our behalf. Many Christians give mental assent to the power and sovereignty of God but do not apply the belief to daily life. Only when we acknowledge and submit to God's control are we moving toward spiritual maturity.

God does not reveal his plans all at once. He wants us to trust that he knows what is best and that no good thing is beyond his ability to deliver. When we submit our desires to God, we lose our craving for control. And that is when we see the plan God has for us begin to unfold.

Submit our lives to scrutiny

Every spiritual community is a microcosm of the entire body of Christ. As we work together, we enjoy the combined wisdom, experience, and talents of all the members. Accountability to other Christians places us in the center of community, which is part of God's plan for his people.

Hank knew he was on the verge of financial disaster, so he struggled and fought to refinance, borrow, and liquidate his assets—anything to solve the problem himself. His freewheeling financial adventures had gotten him in trouble, and he nearly had an emotional breakdown trying to get himself out. When Hank reached the end of his resources, he finally surrendered his situation to God. He knew he needed to let go of his wheeling-and-dealing habits and follow a more sane financial course. He also knew he had to submit himself to the authority of someone who would keep tabs on him. Through his church he found a group of Christian businessmen who agreed to help him.

Five years after his brush with financial disaster, Hank had fully recovered. Then little by little he began taking risks again. One night he awoke in a sweat, realizing that he had reverted to old habits. That morning he called his accountability group and asked the men to meet him for breakfast.

As he confessed his recent transactions, they looked at each other in dismay. Hank had taken some very foolish risks, and they were shocked. "We should have been more assertive in keeping an eye on you," they told him. "This could have gotten out of hand very quickly."

Fortunately, it wasn't too late. The five men worked together to solve Hank's latest escapades. Then they prayed with him and tried to show him from God's Word how greed and pride had tripped him up. They confessed, too, that they had not been as diligent as they might have been. "It's not just a matter of your being accountable to us," one of the men said. "It's a matter of our being responsible friends to you. We'll all have to work a little harder at this."

Voluntary participation in the Christian community and, more specifically, in small accountability groups, is our best guard against living in the secrecy of sin. As we commit ourselves to others, we exchange confidences and create a system of checks and balances. We also gain the spiritual support of prayer, comfort, and encouragement. There is great consolation in knowing that others are praying for us.

Of course, accountability requires humility. To benefit from the experiences and failures of others, we have to learn to listen. We have to stop talking long enough to hear. And we have to set aside our pride, choosing instead to admit, "I've got a lot to learn, and I think you can teach me some valuable lessons." As each member of Christ's body takes this posture of humility, the entire body is built up.

An ancient Hebrew proverb assures us that it is wise to seek the guidance of others: "Plans go wrong for lack of advice; many advisers bring success" (Proverbs 15:22).

Other than willful determination to continue doing what God says we ought not do, pride is the most common reason for not submitting to accountability. Apart from our vanity (and, of course, sin), we have little to lose in listening to others and availing ourselves of their wisdom.

Persevere in Obedience

Every spring, tulip and daffodil bulbs push with all their stored-up strength against the cold dirt packed around them until finally their fragrant, fragile heads poke through the crusty snow. And every child who enters the world does so by pushing against its mother to forge an independent identity. Growth is always *against* something, and spiritual growth is no different. It takes place in a world opposed to God, and it happens among people who are apathetic, indifferent, and sometimes belligerent. Those who follow God are always going against culture. This was true in the days of the patriarchs, it was true in the first century, it is true today, and it will remain true until Christ returns to rule the earth.

To preserve spiritual gains and persevere in faith, we must be prepared to swim against the natural flow of things, for working against us are three powerful forces: our enemy the devil, our enemy ourselves, and our enemy the world.

Our enemy the devil—temptation

Satan has three basic strategies that he uses over and over. Although he adapts them for different people in different situations, he hasn't updated them much since his encounter with Eve in the Garden of Eden. First, he tempts us to doubt

God. Then he suggests that we test God. And finally he implies that he, not God, can give us what we need. He's used these tactics so often and for so long that by now we should laugh in his face when he tries them on us. Sadly, however, Satan seems to be the one doing most of the laughing. He is still deceiving us because we would rather believe sensationalized depictions of him as a repulsive, foul-smelling, fire-breathing monster than as the beautiful creature Scripture states that he is.

The temptation to doubt God

The serpent's words to Eve in the Garden of Eden were intended to cause her to doubt God's goodness; they implied that God was being selfish. "Did God really say you must not eat the fruit from any of the trees in the garden?" the serpent asked (Genesis 3:1). Notice how similar those words are to the ones spoken by the devil to Jesus in the desert. Satan said, "If you are the Son of God, tell these stones to become loaves of bread" (Matthew 4:3). Both statements hint that God is withholding something good. They also imply that it is always bad to be without something we believe would be good to have.

In Eve's case, the serpent implied that being without one particular fruit proved that God was selfish. In Jesus' case, the devil implied that being without food was an unacceptable condition for the one claiming to be the Son of God. In other words, Satan wants us to believe that we shouldn't have to go without whatever it is that we happen to want at any given moment. (And of course he steers us away from any thought that the thing we want could actually be bad for us.)

The temptation to test God

Once doubt has created a crack, human nature urges us to go searching for proof to patch it up. There are two ways of proving God—obedience and disobedience. The way God approves, obviously, is obedience, but that is not the way most people choose. Nor is it the way Satan suggests. Instead of advising Eve to prove God's goodness by obeying God's instructions, he urged her to test her own definition of goodness by being disobedient. Then, after casting doubt on God, he had the audacity to recommend that she put her life at risk to test God. Interesting, isn't it, that he risked nothing to prove himself?

After planting the idea that God was withholding something good, Satan then implied that God cannot be trusted. "You won't die!" the serpent said to the woman (Genesis 3:4). Again, compare this statement to the words spoken by the devil to Jesus: "If you are the Son of God, jump off! For the Scriptures say, 'He will order his angels to protect you. And they will hold you up with their hands so you won't even hurt your foot on a stone'" (Matthew 4:6). To both Eve and Jesus, the enemy was saying, "Make God prove his deity to you." And in so doing, he asked them to discount all the proof God had already given. Interesting, isn't it, that he offered no proof of his own?

The temptation to believe Satan

In his final appeal to Eve, Satan implied that he held the secret to getting the good that he claimed God was keeping for himself. "God knows that your eyes will be opened as soon as you eat it, and you will be like God, knowing both good and evil," he said to Eve (Genesis 3:5). Compare this to the strategy the devil used with Jesus after taking him to a very high mountain and showing him all the kingdoms of the world. "I will give it all to you," the devil said, "if you will kneel down and worship me" (Matthew 4:9).

At this point, naive Eve made the choice we've all made countless times. She chose to trust her own senses rather than God. She saw that the fruit was good for food, pleasing to look at, and desirable for gaining wisdom, so she took some and ate it (see Genesis 3:6).

With three leading (or *mis*leading) statements, the serpent convinced Eve that he could do for her what God could not or would not do, and all creation has been suffering the consequences ever since.

Jesus, on the other hand, dismissed Satan with words from the Torah. "Get out of here, Satan," Jesus told him. "For the Scriptures say, 'You must worship the Lord your God and serve only him'" (Matthew 4:10). And by so doing, Jesus spared us from the eternal consequences of our sin. Eve's doubt led to disobedience and death for the world; Christ's belief resulted in obedience and life for the world.[2]

Eve had the closest thing to a perfect situation any human this side of eternity will ever know, yet she allowed herself to crave something more. Her "if only" thinking led her to take something God did not want her to have. Christ reversed this kind of thinking. He too had a desire that did not match God's—he wanted to be spared the horror of Roman crucifixion. But Jesus, instead of saying "if only," said, "only if." He asked God to spare him from the agony *only if* it would fit God's plan and accomplish his purpose.

As a result of Eve's "if only" thinking, she and Adam were banished from the garden, the gates were locked behind them (figuratively speaking), and angelic guards with flaming swords were sent to guard the entrance. In contrast, Christ's "only if" thinking provided the keys that unlock the doors to God's heavenly Kingdom. After Peter's profession of faith in Jesus as Messiah, Jesus said to him, "I will give you the keys of the Kingdom of Heaven. Whatever you forbid on earth will be forbidden in heaven, and whatever you permit on earth will be permitted in heaven" (Matthew 16:19).

Our enemy, ourselves—weakness

People often confuse weakness with sinfulness, but being weak is not a sin; it is simply a fact of being human. Our strength, like our knowledge, is limited for one simple reason: we are not God. Human beings have been weak since the beginning, and it is not due to a flaw in God's design; it is part of his original plan. We are made to be in relationship with God and to receive our strength from him. Weakness does, however, become a factor in sin when we try to satisfy our desires in defiance of God or apart from his involvement.

In perhaps the most famous passage of Scripture on the subject of human weakness, the apostle Paul laments his lack of power over sin:

> I don't really understand myself, for I want to do what is right, but I don't do it. Instead, I do what I hate. But if I know that what I am doing is wrong, this shows that I agree that the law is good. So I am not the one doing wrong; it is sin living in me that does it.
>
> And I know that nothing good lives in me, that is, in my sinful nature. I want to do what is right, but I can't. I want to do what is good, but I don't. I don't want to do what is wrong, but I do it anyway. But if I do what I don't want to do, I am not really the one doing wrong; it is sin living in me that does it.
>
> I have discovered this principle of life—that when I want to do what is right, I inevitably do what is wrong. I love God's law with all my heart. But there is another power within me that is at war with my mind. This power makes me a slave to the sin that is still within me. Oh, what a miserable person I am! Who will free me from this life that is dominated by sin and death? Thank God! The answer is in Jesus Christ our Lord. So you see how it is: In my mind I really want to obey God's law, but because of my sinful nature I am a slave to sin. Romans 7:15-25

From this confession we learn that the apostle's useful-ness to God was not based on his strength; it was based on his acknowledgement of weakness and on his ongoing strug-gle to get the desires of his heart, mind, and body aligned with God.

In contrast, we often try instead to align God with our desires. Take John, for example. In speaking of a coworker with whom he's become friends, John said, "Beth is the best friend I've ever had. My wife just criticizes me all the time, but Beth understands me and accepts me—even all my flaws. I can't believe that a loving God would ask me to give up a relationship with such a wonderful person."

And Sue. "The only place I ever feel accepted is in a bar," Sue said. "My drinking friends accept me for who I am, just the way I am. They don't care how I look. They make me feel like one of them. I never feel that kind of love at church."

John and Sue, in their separate ways, express the longing of every human heart. While wisdom was the bait that Eve fell for, love and acceptance are the lures that hook people in our era. Unconditional love is everyone's inner desire, and the acceptance offered by the world is indeed an enticing counterfeit. The "goodness" of such acceptance is debat-able, however. Acceptance that leaves us wallowing in weakness and tries to make us feel good about failure is more of a curse than a blessing. Acceptance may make us feel good about who we are, but it can give us neither the incentive nor the power to become better than we were.

There's no denying the allure of the world's version of love; it offers everything and demands nothing. But this has appeal only because we don't yet see the world with God's eyes. We don't see it the way it could and should be. We don't see it the way God created it and wants it to be. Our eyes are still dim and our thinking is still foggy if we believe we can have anything good apart from God and his original plan.

Our enemy the world—persecution

Jesus spent three years pouring his life into the twelve men he called disciples. He taught them about God's new covenant, showed them how to live, and gave them authority to do miracles in his name. Then came time for last-minute instructions, for he was about to leave them. Though his work on earth was ending, theirs was just beginning.

Jesus didn't motivate them with tales of adventure and excitement. He didn't send them off with a pep talk about positive thinking. Nor did he promise them early retirement in a seaside community. He sent them off with this ominous warning: "Look, I am sending you out as sheep among wolves" (Matthew 10:16). Jesus protected them from future doubt, disappointment, and despair by preparing them for what was to come. And he did so by teaching them truth and warning them of persecution.

The apostle John later wrote about how people responded to the difficult teachings of Jesus. According to his account, many disciples "turned away and deserted him" after Jesus finished teaching (John 6:66). That brief statement tells us that many of those who heard Christ's words, walked in his footsteps, and witnessed his miracles turned away and went home when they found out that he wasn't promising them health, prosperity, and political freedom.

Jesus' warning was not a false alarm. A short time after his resurrection, the situation between Hebrew believers and nonbelievers heated up. The Hebrew Christians were being publicly humiliated, ridiculed, beaten, thrown into jail, and their property was being confiscated. And yet they were commended and encouraged to persevere. The letter written to them says,

Think back on those early days when you first learned about Christ. Remember how you remained faithful even though it meant terrible suffering. Sometimes you were exposed to public ridicule and were beaten, and sometimes you helped others who were suffering the same things. You suffered along with those who were thrown into jail, and when all you owned was taken from you, you accepted it with joy. You knew there were better things waiting for you that will last forever.

So do not throw away this confident trust in the Lord. Remember the great reward it brings you! Patient endurance is what you need now, so that you will continue to do God's will. Then you will receive all that he has promised.

Hebrews 10:32-36

Few American Christians experience physical persecution; we are more often subjected to the psychological varieties like scorn and ridicule. But people around the world are experiencing persecution even as I write.

Daniel is a young Nigerian who declared his belief in Jesus. Soon after making his decision, he returned to his Muslim village, excited about telling his friends and neighbors. His news was not met with favor, however. Furious at his conversion, the women beat him and left him for dead in the bushes. When he regained consciousness the following day, he decided he must not have been clear in his witness. So he went back to the village and witnessed again. And again the women beat him and left him for dead. This time he remained unconscious for two days. When he awoke, he again assumed that he had not expressed himself well. So he returned the third time. This time the village women broke into tears at his perseverance, and eventually the gospel gained a foothold in that place.

We may never experience the kind of physical persecution Daniel and others have suffered and continue to suffer in some places, but all of us will at some time be in a situation where believing in Jesus will be a considerable disadvantage. Our response at such a time is the measure of our spiritual condition. If we cannot even persevere during times of persecution that is not life threatening, we are foolish to assume we will have the strength to withstand threats against our lives.

If the first followers turned away from the Son of God after seeing him, hearing him, and touching him, none of us should presume that we are immune to the temptations and pressures at work in a world opposed to God.

Although we cannot always avoid temptation, we can reduce our vulnerability to it by saturating our minds with truth so that Satan's words will sound ludicrous to us; although we cannot completely conquer our weakness, we can avail ourselves of Christ's strength; and although we cannot escape persecution, we can develop endurance in minor adversity so that we'll be strong enough to persevere even when our lives are on the line.

Our task as believers is to carry on the work started by Jesus and continued by his disciples and the apostles. To do this, we must protect ourselves spiritually. The Bible outlines a clear plan for doing so.

Our Strategy

God and Satan are engaged in ongoing conflict, and those who choose Christ's side join an army unlike any other. It is an army that does battle with spiritual weapons. Unless we learn to use them, we will be sitting ducks for Satan's subtle strategies; he will use every trick he knows to frighten us into retreat or lure us over to his side.

Our strategy is threefold: put on spiritual armor, produce spiritual fruit, and practice spiritual disciplines.

Put on spiritual armor

To guard our spiritual well-being, we must first put on protective covering. Paul wrote about this in his letter to the believers in the city of Ephesus, the capital of the Roman province of Asia:

> Put on every piece of God's armor so you will be able to resist the enemy in the time of evil. Then after the battle you will still be standing firm. Stand your ground, putting on the belt of *truth* and the body armor of God's *righteousness*. For shoes, put on the *peace* that comes from the Good News so that you will be fully prepared. In addition to all of these, hold up the shield of *faith* to stop the fiery arrows of the devil. Put on *salvation* as your helmet, and take the sword of the Spirit, which is the word of God.
>
> Ephesians 6:13-17 (italics added)

Truth: protection from deceit

Deceit is particularly dangerous because it can camouflage a lie so well that we, in ignorance or naïveté, can be absolutely convinced that it is true. Look at the number of people today who are absolutely convinced that abortion is better than an "unwanted" child, that stealing is better than going without a certain kind of shoes, or that lying is better than acknowledging weakness or wrongdoing. Satan's most successful use of deceit comes in the form of this lie: "If you want it, it is good." He will never tell us that the thing we want is bad for us, no matter how deadly it may be, because he wants us to become slaves to our desires, for then we will be useless to God.

Righteousness: protection from evil

"Fight fire with fire" is the world's method of self-protection. But God advises the opposite. Jesus said, "Do not resist an evil person! If someone slaps you on the right cheek, offer the other cheek also" (Matthew 5:39).

Before baseball player Jackie Robinson was allowed to join the all-white major league, he was asked what he would do if another player hit him across the cheek. Robinson replied, "Sir, I have two cheeks." Based on his answer, Robinson was allowed to enter the league because officials knew that he had the strength of character to absorb the blows of injustice, not perpetuate it.

Peace: our protection from Satan

"In the Bible, shalom means universal flourishing, wholeness, and delight—a rich state of affairs in which natural needs are satisfied and natural gifts fruitfully employed, a state of affairs that inspires joyful wonder as its Creator and Savior opens doors and welcomes the creatures in whom he delights. Shalom, in other words, is the way things ought to be."[3] The Good News can be summarized in one simple word: *peace.* That gospel is all we need to ward off Satan and his accusers, because peace is the antithesis of all Satan represents.

Faith: protection from doubt

Faith is essential to Christianity, but faith in God is not enough. The book of James says: "You say you have faith, for you believe that there is one God. Good for you! Even the demons believe this, and they tremble in terror. How foolish! Can't you see that faith without good deeds is useless?" (James 2:19-20). In addition to believing *in* God, we must also believe everything God says about how to live. As we learned earlier, doubt is the "fiery arrow" that Satan aims at us. And faith proven through confident obedience is the only reliable defense against doubt.

Salvation: protection from sin and death

In Paul's second letter to Timothy, he wrote: "And now he has made all of this plain to us by the appearing of Christ

Jesus, our Savior. He broke the power of death and illuminated the way to life and immortality through the Good News" (2 Timothy 1:10). When Christ died to sin, we died with him. When he conquered death and sin by rising from the dead, we too gained the victory. Paul explained it to the Romans this way:

> Our old sinful selves were crucified with Christ so that sin might lose its power in our lives. We are no longer slaves to sin. For when we died with Christ we were set free from the power of sin. And since we died with Christ, we know we will also live with him. We are sure of this because Christ was raised from the dead, and he will never die again. Death no longer has any power over him. When he died, he died once to break the power of sin. But now that he lives, he lives for the glory of God. So you also should consider yourselves to be dead to the power of sin and alive to God through Christ Jesus.   Romans 6:6-11

When we choose to follow Jesus, sin doesn't immediately lose its appeal to us; it simply loses its power over us. Until God gives us glorified bodies, we will remain not only susceptible to sin but also inclined toward it. That is why we need to watch our ways. If we continually choose sin, we will suffer the consequences of broken peace, damaged relationships, and lost joy. But if we continue to pursue spiritual renewal, our lives will become whole and fruitful.

Produce spiritual fruit

People visiting the eastern shore of the Sea of Galilee prior to 1967 saw a peculiar sight: Israeli farmers going about their work in very odd-looking machines. To protect themselves from mortar shells thrown down by Syrian soldiers stationed high above them in the controversial Golan Heights, the farmers had to work in armored tractors. These farmers didn't need any agricultural experts to tell them that they couldn't produce much fruit if they didn't first protect their own lives.

Unfortunately, we are not so wise when it comes to our spiritual lives. We expect to produce a harvest of spiritual fruit without first protecting ourselves against enemy attack. Without the spiritual protection spoken of above, our attempts to produce an abundant crop of spiritual fruit are doomed to failure.

In some Christian circles, producing spiritual fruit is thought to be the same as producing new converts. But that is not the way the apostle Paul spoke of it. He said the fruit of the Spirit is "love, joy, peace, patience, kindness, goodness, faithfulness, gentleness, and self-control" (Galatians 5:22-23). These are the qualities we reap when we sow seeds of godliness. Evangelism may be a by-product, but it is not the primary result. True spiritual fruit is not a behavior we learn nor a duty we perform. It is the product of a loving relationship with the Son of God. As Jesus said, "Remain in me, and I will remain in you. For a branch cannot produce fruit if it is severed from the vine, and you cannot be fruitful unless you remain in me. Yes, I am the vine; you are the branches. Those who remain in me, and I in them, will produce much fruit. For apart from me you can do nothing" (John 15:4-5).

This type of fruit does not grow naturally; it has to be planted in well-prepared soil, nurtured with regular watering and weeding, and pruned to get rid of dead, nonproducing branches. But the result is well worth the effort, for "the one who sows to please the Spirit, from the Spirit will reap eternal life" (Galatians 6:8, NIV).

Practice spiritual disciplines

The word *discipline* often causes us to put up our defenses because of its close association with the idea of punishment.

This is unfortunate because an accurate definition of discipline includes teaching, instruction, and tutoring. In other words, discipline is "training or experience that corrects, molds, strengthens, or perfects, especially the mental faculties or moral character."[4]

This type of discipline is as appropriate for saints as it is for sinners. Whether we are children or adults, single or married, business people or clergy, we all have the same human nature and therefore the same human needs. If the perfect Son of God needed to practice spiritual disciplines, surely the imperfect sons of men need to practice them even more. One of the best guarantees for ongoing spiritual growth, therefore, is to live as Christ lived. Dallas Willard, in his popular book *The Spirit of the Disciplines*, wrote:

> If we have faith in Christ, we must believe that he knew how to live. We can, through faith and grace, become like Christ by practicing the types of activities he engaged in, by arranging our whole lives around the activities he himself practiced in order to remain constantly at home in the fellowship of his Father.
>
> What activities did Jesus practice? Such things as solitude and silence, prayer, simple and sacrificial living, intense study and meditation upon God's Word and God's ways, and service to others. . . . In a balanced life of such activities, we will be constantly enlivened by "The Kingdom Not of This World"—the Kingdom of Truth as seen in John 18:36-37.[5]

Spiritual disciplines are the practices that protect our faith. Paul described them in his first letter to Timothy: "Train yourself to be godly. Physical training is good, but training for godliness is much better, promising benefits in this life and in the life to come" (1 Timothy 4:7-8).

Spiritual disciplines fall into two general categories: *abstaining from* and *adding to*. "Put to death" is the phrase

Paul used to express the idea of abstinence (Colossians 3:5). He also used the phrases "putting off" or "taking off" the old nature. Paul said, "Don't lie to each other, for you have *stripped off* your old sinful nature and all its wicked deeds" (Colossians 3:9, italics added). Peter described the same thing when he wrote, "Dear friends, I warn you as 'temporary residents and foreigners' to *keep away from* worldly desires that wage war against your very souls" (1 Peter 2:11, italics added).

The other type of spiritual discipline involves taking positive action, that is, by *adding to* or *putting on* something. Paul said to "*put on* all of God's armor so that you will be able to stand firm against all strategies of the devil" (Ephesians 6:11, italics added). Writing to the Colossians, Paul continued this theme, saying, "*Put on* the new self, which is being renewed in knowledge in the image of its Creator" (Colossians 3:10, NIV, italics added). Again, Paul urged believers to "*put on* the shining armor of right living" (Romans 13:12, italics added).

Using this distinction, we can list the disciplines like this:

PUTTING ON	PUTTING OFF (abstinence)
Prayer	Giving/Stewardship
Study/Meditation	Solitude
Worship	Fasting
Service	Confession
Spiritual Freedom	Silence

This list is not exhaustive. These are simply some of the more common ones. A scriptural study of each one will bring into focus a clear picture of how to exercise them.[6]

The practice of spiritual disciplines will change our hearts, our minds, and our lives. It also will make us more effective in ministering to others and thereby continuing the process of redemption, both in our own lives and in the lives of those to whom God sends us.

Moses found this to be true. Forty years of solitude as a shepherd in Midian prepared him for his ultimate calling: to become the shepherd of the people of Israel and to lead them out of captivity.

Moses had a choice in life that few others have. He could have remained a member of the royal, ruling family or become one of their slaves. Going against every human inclination, Moses chose the latter. His God-given passion for justice led him to identify with the oppressed rather than the oppressors. According to the writer of Hebrews, Moses "refused to be called the son of Pharaoh's daughter. He chose to share the oppression of God's people instead of enjoying the fleeting pleasures of sin. He thought it was better to suffer for the sake of Christ than to own the treasures of Egypt, for he was looking ahead to his great reward" (Hebrews 11:24-26).

When Moses made this choice, he had no way of knowing the place in biblical history he would gain. Nor did he know that he would be remembered for centuries as a righteous man; he simply knew it was the right thing to do at the time. By doing this, Moses identified himself with God, and as a result of his obedience, this is what God said about him:

> Never since has there arisen a prophet in Israel like
> Moses, whom the LORD knew face to face. He was
> unequaled for all the signs and wonders that the LORD
> sent him to perform in the land of Egypt, against Pharaoh
> and all his servants and his entire land, and for all the

mighty deeds and all the terrifying displays of power that
Moses performed in the sight of all Israel.

Deuteronomy 34:10-12, NRSV

At one time or another we all will have a person (or situation) in our lives like Moses had in Pharaoh, someone or something that hinders us from doing what we know God wants us to do. However, none of us ever will be in a position where it is impossible to do God's will. There is no such place! Even though we may be unable to get others to cooperate, we always have a choice. We can identify either with God's people or with his enemies; we can either continue struggling against evil or give up. That is the difference between being in God's will and out of it. If we pursue God in the face of persecution and obey God despite opposition, we are persevering, protecting our spiritual well-being, and that is God's will for each of us. "God blesses those who patiently endure testing and temptation. Afterward they will receive the crown of life that God has promised to those who love him" (James 1:12).

Notes

1. Philip Yancey, "Nietzsche Was Right," *Books & Culture* (January/February 1998): 14.

2. The section on temptation is adapted from "The Perfect Cover-Up" by Julie Ackerman Link, *Seasons* (Spring 1998): 9. Used by permission.

3. Cornelius Plantinga Jr., *Not the Way It's Supposed to Be: A Breviary of Sin* (Grand Rapids, Mich.: Eerdmans, 1995), 10.

4. *Webster's Third New International Dictionary of the English Language*, unabridged (Springfield, Mass.: Merriam-Webster, Inc., 1986).

5. Dallas Willard, *The Spirit of the Disciplines: Understanding How God Changes Lives* (San Francisco: Harper & Row, 1988), ix–x.

6. *The Spiritual Renewal Bible* includes a series of devotionals on these spiritual disciplines. Other helpful books on the subject include the following: Richard Foster, *The Celebration of Discipline: The Path to Spiritual Growth*; Dallas Willard, *The Spirit of the Disciplines*; David Stoop, *Seeking God Together: Spiritual Intimacy in Marriage*; Douglas J. Rumford, *SoulShaping: Taking Care of Your Spiritual Life through Godly Disciplines*.

START TODAY!

How to Preserve Spiritual Gains
- Participate in Christian fellowship
- Make yourself accountable to other Christians to obey God
- Persevere when times are difficult
- Inherit God's promises through faith and obedience
- Put on spiritual armor
- Produce spiritual fruit
- Practice spiritual disciplines
- Swim against the current of ungodly cultural influences
- Seek godly counsel in your decision making

BIBLICAL EXAMPLE
Moses leading the children of Israel

BIBLE VERSES
Hebrews 10:35-36: "Do not throw away this confident trust in the Lord. Remember the great reward it brings you! Patient endurance is what you need now, so that you will continue to do God's will. Then you will receive all that he has promised."

Chapter 8
Following Jesus, Loving God

I want them to be encouraged and knit together
by strong ties of love.
I want them to have complete confidence
that they understand God's mysterious plan,
which is Christ himself.
In him lie hidden all the treasures of wisdom and knowledge.

Colossians 2:2-3

Though the LORD is very great and lives in heaven,
he will make Jerusalem his home of justice and righteousness.
In that day he will be your sure foundation,
providing a rich store of salvation, wisdom, and knowledge.
The fear of the LORD will be your treasure.

Isaiah 33:5-6

THE RELIGIOUS Jews were divided on many things, but the one thing they agreed on was Jesus. He was a nuisance, and they wanted him out of their way. His preaching was attracting too many followers, his teaching was causing too much controversy and his miracles were causing too much disruption. To put it simply, they were jealous; Jesus was getting all too much attention, and they wanted to get rid of him.

So the religious leaders took turns trying to trap Jesus into saying something that would contradict Moses' law.

One day while Jesus was teaching in the temple, the chief priests and Pharisees hung around watching and listening for an excuse to arrest him. Jesus' stories were aimed against them; that much they knew. But they didn't dare touch him because the people considered him a prophet. So they waited. They listened. They debated. And finally they came up with a question they thought would force Jesus into a corner. "Is it right to pay taxes to the Roman government or not?" they asked.

Knowing they were trying to trick him, Jesus asked to see the Roman coin used to pay the tax.

"Whose picture is on this coin?" Jesus asked.

"Caesar's," they answered.

"Then give to Caesar what belongs to him and to God what belongs to God" (adapted from Matthew 22:15-22).

The question they hoped would put Jesus into a theological corner placed them there instead. With his surprisingly simple but straightforward answer, Jesus moved himself out of the light of suspicion and put his questioners into it. This display of power amazed those listening as much as if Jesus had physically traded places with the Pharisees. The people were unaccustomed to seeing self-righteous religious leaders put on the spot.

For the religious leaders themselves, the challenge was as humiliating as it was surprising, and they trudged off amazed and muttering.

Later the same day the Sadducees, another religious group, came along and used the same tactic. Another trick question. This time the question centered on a convoluted, hypothetical story.

Again Jesus responded in a way that amazed the crowd and left the religious leaders shaking their heads.

After hearing that the Sadducees had also failed to trap Jesus, the Pharisees decided to try one more time.

The question they thought would surely silence Jesus was this: "Of all the commandments, which is the most important?"

Without hesitation, Jesus answered: "'Listen, O Israel! The LORD our God is the one and only LORD. And you must love the LORD your God with all your heart, all your soul, all your mind, and all your strength.' The second is equally important: 'Love your neighbor as yourself.' No other commandment is greater than these" (Mark 12:28-31).

Their strategy failed again. Jesus gave them an answer straight from the law of Moses—an answer they couldn't dispute without calling into question their own spiritual sincerity.

The answer Jesus gave long ago remains true today, and it is a perfect guideline for us to follow as we learn to use the concepts presented in this book. The five categories Jesus mentioned—heart, soul, mind, strength, and relationships—touch every area of life that we pollute and pervert through bad choices and wrong behavior. Whenever we allow feelings, desires, thoughts, habits, or relationships to be directed or motivated by anything other than love for God, they begin working against us and we begin the agonizing process of self-destruction.

When we ignore God, we end up locked in a room with no view, isolated from the world and people we love, threatened by enemies we can neither see nor identify, unable to see where we've gone wrong, and therefore ignorant as to how to make things right.

This is the inevitable result when we go where we have no business going, do things we ought not to be doing, slam doors that should be left open, become angry when the doors we close are locked behind us, and blame others for locking us out. Sadly, this is also the inevitable result when we're in a relationship with someone who does such things.

Each area of life is like a room. When the door of a room is locked, we're prevented from making spiritual progress. Many people, for example, find a dead bolt on the room of relationships. They get stuck over and over in a relationship with a particular person (perhaps a mother-in-law) or in certain kinds of relationships (perhaps with those in authority).

Examining the events that lead to these locked rooms will help us determine which keys will open the locks. Different keys work in different locks. If you are in a locked relationship with your mother-in-law, the key you may need is the one labeled "Take responsibility." Instead of focusing on everything she does to shut you out, begin taking responsibility for what you do that makes her want to slam the door. Or you may need to see the truth of the situation, admit wrongdoing, take responsibility, and ask forgiveness.

Some doors have numerous locks that require several keys, but seldom does a single situation require every key. Sometimes it's necessary to try several keys before finding the one that fits. Although we introduced the seven concepts in sequential order, they need not be used that way.

Whenever we find ourselves locked in a situation we can't get out of—due either to our own bad choices or someone else's—we need to figure out which area (or areas) of life has the lock on it, determine which of the spiritual keys will open it, and begin using them. The chart on the next page is a guideline to use. Check the boxes that apply to you. Then, as you read this chapter, circle the keys you need to begin using.

The stories in the following sections are based on true circumstances. Put yourself in each situation and try to figure out which keys would unlock doors to spiritual progress. In

"Love God with Your . . ."

HEART (FEELINGS)	LOCKS	SPIRITUAL KEYS
	▪ Fear	1. Seek God and Surrender to Him
	▪ Anxiety	2. See the Truth
	▪ Panic	3. Speak the Truth
	▪ Other	4. Take Responsibility
		5. Grieve, Forgive, and Let Go
		6. Transform Your Life
		7. Preserve Spiritual Gains!

SOUL (DESIRES)	LOCKS	SPIRITUAL KEYS
	▪ Power	1. Seek God and Surrender to Him
	▪ Prestige	2. See the Truth
	▪ Possessions	3. Speak the Truth
	▪ Other	4. Take Responsibility
		5. Grieve, Forgive, and Let Go
		6. Transform Your Life
		7. Preserve Spiritual Gains!

MIND (THOUGHTS)	LOCKS	SPIRITUAL KEYS
	▪ Discouragement	1. Seek God and Surrender to Him
	▪ Disillusionment	2. See the Truth
	▪ Depression	3. Speak the Truth
	▪ Other	4. Take Responsibility
		5. Grieve, Forgive, and Let Go
		6. Transform Your Life
		7. Preserve Spiritual Gains!

STRENGTH (HABITS)	LOCKS	SPIRITUAL KEYS
	▪ Addictions	1. Seek God and Surrender to Him
	▪ Compulsions	2. See the Truth
	▪ Obsessions	3. Speak the Truth
	▪ Other	4. Take Responsibility
		5. Grieve, Forgive, and Let Go
		6. Transform Your Life
		7. Preserve Spiritual Gains!

AND YOUR NEIGHBOR AS YOURSELF (RELATIONSHIPS)	LOCKS	SPIRITUAL KEYS
	▪ Dependency	1. Seek God and Surrender to Him
	▪ Estrangement	2. See the Truth
	▪ Impropriety	3. Speak the Truth
	▪ Other	4. Take Responsibility
		5. Grieve, Forgive, and Let Go
		6. Transform Your Life
		7. Preserve Spiritual Gains!

the margins of this book (or in a separate notebook) write which keys ought to be used. Get in the habit of thinking about how to use these concepts in everyday life.

Feelings: Loving God with My Heart

Gina was feeling especially anxious, so she got on her knees and pleaded for God's peace. Immediately her mind wandered to several tasks she needed to complete. She tried to focus on prayer, but a sudden flood of fear washed over her as she thought about unpaid bills, unfulfilled responsibilities, and her vulnerable, adolescent children. She tried again to focus on God. But once again her anxieties intruded. Gina moved from her knees to a prone position. Flat on her face, she prayed, "God, help me! I can't even concentrate well enough to pray!" She tried to calm herself, but her body refused to relax. Then she remembered what seemed to be a random and unrelated incident.

The previous summer, Gina and a friend had gone snorkeling in the waters off Catalina Island. Excited about viewing the colorful fish and plants thriving in the crystalline Pacific water, Gina had pulled on her fins and mask and eased into the tide. But immediately she began kicking, gasping, and flailing in the water. For an hour, she tried desperately to stay afloat.

Her friend, an experienced swimmer and scuba diver, was nearby, and Gina marveled at the ease with which she moved through the water. She managed to stay afloat by casually moving her arms and occasionally kicking her feet, which allowed her to concentrate on the glorious undersea gardens. Gina got only a glimpse of one bright orange fish and a cloud of silvery minnows because her full attention was fixed on staying afloat.

As Gina reviewed the scene, she realized what God was trying to tell her. She had refused to trust what he had provided for her safety—the natural buoyancy of the salt water to keep her afloat, the swim fins to keep her moving, and the snorkeling tube to enable her to breathe. Instead she kicked and fought to keep from drowning. But all her flailing had not saved her; it had just kept her from enjoying the beauty all around her.

Gina was doing the same thing now, she realized. Instead of trusting God, she was frantically kicking and splashing to save herself. Intellectually, Gina had surrendered herself to God. But emotionally and practically she had not, and her lack of trust was causing emotional turmoil. There was no real threat to her life. There was simply an accumulation of concerns that seemed like a flood she had no power to stop.

Scripture addresses the problem of fear with sixty-five admonitions that say, "Do not be afraid." But simply being told not to do something leaves us far short of knowing how not to do it. And even the diligent reading of all sixty-five Scripture verses won't move us much closer to practical knowledge. There is, however, one thing that will help. A study of the character of God reveals the reasons we need never be afraid. Here are a few: "The LORD your God is gracious and merciful. If you return to him, he will not continue to turn his face from you" (2 Chronicles 30:9). "The LORD is my rock, my fortress, and my savior; my God is my rock, in whom I find protection. He is my shield, the power that saves me, and my place of safety" (Psalm 18:2). "My health may fail, and my spirit may grow weak, but God remains the strength of my heart; he is mine forever" (Psalm 73:26).

Perhaps the most assuring Scripture we can find are the words of Jesus himself, who said, "I am leaving you with a gift—peace of mind and heart. And the peace I give is a gift the world cannot give. So don't be troubled or afraid" (John 14:27).

When the One who created us, knows us, and loves us says, "Don't be afraid," we can have confidence that the advice is reliable. And when we have intimate knowledge of the One who says it, we have additional evidence that we can trust it.

The apostle Paul had the kind of intimate knowledge we're talking about. In fact, he had such confidence that he wrote this to the believers in Philippi:

> Don't worry about anything; instead, pray about everything. Tell God what you need, and thank him for all he has done. Then you will experience God's peace, which exceeds anything we can understand. His peace will guard your hearts and minds as you live in Christ Jesus.　　Philippians 4:6-7

According to Paul, God's way for us to deal with fear and worry is fourfold: First, stop long enough to take stock of the situation. Second, thank God for his promise to meet all our needs. Third, find the legitimate need hidden beneath the anxiety. Fourth, present the real need to God as a request.

When we deal with anxieties according to God's instructions, God gives results. And when we turn our anxieties into specific petitions, offered in grateful prayer, the result will be peace that is beyond human understanding.

On two occasions Jesus addressed worry and anxiety in his followers by asking a question. One time was in a boat with his disciples, and the other time was at the empty tomb. These two questions get to the heart of every "heart problem."

In a well-known Bible story about a life-threatening storm on the Sea of Galilee, Jesus posed this probing question to his frightened followers as the wind roared, the seas rolled, and the ship rocked: "Where is your faith?" Their response came in the form of another question, one that revealed the hidden reason for their fear and anxiety. They said to one another, "Who is this man, that even the winds and waves obey him?" (See Luke 8:22-25.)

Their answer to the question Jesus asked revealed that their faith was in the wrong things. They were trusting their knowledge of the sea and their own sailing abilities, both of which were now proving inadequate; they were not trusting Jesus. And why not? Because, as they themselves admitted, they didn't yet realize who he was.

In another familiar biblical scene we see Mary at the empty tomb of Jesus, weeping because his body is gone. Walking up behind her, the resurrected Christ asks this two-in-one question: "Why are you crying? Who are you looking for?" Not recognizing Jesus and thinking he was the gardener, Mary asked him to tell her where he had put the body of Jesus. Her response was similar to that of the disciples. While their faith was *in* the wrong thing, Mary was looking *for* the wrong thing. She was so desperate to find a dead body that she almost missed seeing a living Savior. (See John 20:11-15.)

Both questions Jesus asked—"Where is your faith?" (Luke 8:25) and "Who are you looking for?" (John 20:15)—have to do with his identity. Neither the disciples nor Mary had yet figured out who Jesus really was.

Most, perhaps all, human fear and worry are due to this one truth: we don't yet know who Jesus is. By honestly answering the questions Jesus asked, we can pinpoint the source of our fear and worry. When we realize that our faith is based on something totally unreliable, we are forced to look for something trustworthy. And when we recognize that we're looking for the wrong thing, our blind eyes can then see the real thing—Jesus.

If your struggle has to do with loving God with your heart, ask yourself these two questions: "Where is my

faith?" and "What am I looking for?" Then determine
which of the spiritual keys will fit the lock on your heart.

Desires: Loving God with My Soul

Murray is an award-winning salesman who earns a six-figure
income year after year. His wife and children are Christians,
and Murray claims to believe everything they tell him about
prayer, peace, and even salvation. But he says he can't afford
to follow Christ because he would have to change his business practices.

One thing we can say about Murray is that he's honest.
He refuses to say he is one thing while behaving like another.

Jesus taught that we cannot serve two masters. Murray
knows that better than some Christians and, in a back-
handed way, is honoring it. He has made a conscious decision to serve money rather than God. His personal ambition
is to acquire wealth and possessions.

Murray represents a large segment of people in our
consumer-driven culture, including some Christians. But
Christians have trouble being honest about it, so they
struggle with the tension of trying to honor two competing
deities.

The love of money has a powerful pull, but it's not the
only desire that squeezes God out of his rightful place.
Alongside the drive to acquire more possessions by accumu-
lating more money are the desires for power, position, and
prestige. Some people are energized by rivalry and can't
imagine living without the surge of adrenaline they feel when
they outwit the competition. Some people crave power over
others and feel insecure unless they are in charge. Some hunger for the prestige of fame and public approval.

We are quick to label insatiable desires for money, sex,
fame, or food as sin, but even "good" desires can lead to
evil if we don't keep them in check with truth. For example,

people who are passionately committed to their families or to church can easily succumb to ambitious motives, arrogant attitudes, and self-serving behavior. One exposure to a group of Little League parents at a close game tells us more than we want to know about parental pride and ambition. Others may genuinely seek to take the light of Christ into a dark world, but because the need is so great, they rationalize unethical fund-raising tactics.

The nature of Christianity is to be caught between good and evil forces as we attempt to fulfill our God-given tasks. Some forces are external, like those placed on us by friends, relatives, coworkers, employers, or church leaders. Others are internal; they are the ones that involve our personal dreams, ambitions, and goals.

Many seek God in times of trouble and surrender the offending piece of their lives for a time but take it back when the crisis is over, still believing they know better than God what will bring them meaning, purpose, and pleasure. If we cannot lay every aspect of life before God without dreading his thorough examination, we have not yet said "It's yours." And we cannot experience spiritual renewal until we have surrendered everything to God—including every desire and ambition.

As we let go of selfish ambitions, God can begin to show us what is behind our drive to achieve and why we hold on so tightly to the things we acquire. Our motivations often remain unknown to us because we don't spend time examining them. Sometimes they are as basic as pride and greed, which may manifest themselves as anything from competitiveness to dishonesty or even theft. But some motives remain well hidden. For example, the fear of deprivation may be a motive that expresses itself in words like these: "I'll never be poor again." Perhaps that vow, even though it was never spoken audibly, is still in control.

When we surrender to God, he begins to reveal an array of motives, goals, and intentions that tell us more about ourselves than most of us want to know. But that greater self-understanding will also show us which spiritual concepts to use. When we see the truth about our motives and agree with God about our values, he can begin changing our desires to match his.

Jesus asked two questions that will help us identify the stubborn lock on our souls.

While walking to Jerusalem with his disciples for the last time, Jesus began revealing what was going to happen to him. Then the mother of James and John, the sons of Zebedee, came to Jesus with her sons.

"What is it you want?" Jesus asked her.

Kneeling in respect, she asked, "In your Kingdom, will you let my two sons sit in places of honor next to you, one at your right and the other at your left?" (See Matthew 20:17-21, NIV.)

In one sense, this mother was being unselfish. She was asking nothing for herself. But her request showed that even though she loved her sons very much, she didn't know enough to ask the right thing for them. Although she was asking for a *good* thing—closeness to Jesus—she was asking for a wrong reason—power and prestige for her sons.

When the lock on your life is an unexamined desire, remember Jesus' question: "What is it you want?" But also remember that the motive behind the answer is as important as the answer itself.

Within a very short time, the events Jesus told them about that day all came true. The betrayal. The arrest. The trial. The torture. And finally the crucifixion. The disciples' dreams of greatness were gone. Their excitement about Jesus' coming kingdom was no more than a bittersweet memory. In despair, the disciples went back to their old occupation—fishing.

One morning they were heading back to shore after working all night and catching nothing. From the beach, a voice called to them.

"Friends, have you caught any fish?"

"No," they answered.

"Then throw your net over the right side and you will find some."

Even though the men knew it was silly to think that fish would be on one side of a small fishing boat and not the other, they followed the instructions. When they did, they were unable to haul in the net because of the large number of fish.

Realizing then that it was Jesus speaking to them, they quickly towed their heavy nets to shore. When they landed, they saw a fire of burning coals with fish on it.

Jesus had made breakfast for them. In a scene reminiscent of the time he had fed five thousand on a nearby hillside, Jesus served them bread and fish.

After they had eaten, Jesus said to Peter, "Do you love me more than these?" (See John 21:4-15.)

Theologians debate what the word *these* means. Some believe Jesus was asking Peter if he loved Jesus more than the other disciples loved him. Others say Jesus was asking Peter if he loved Jesus more than he loved the other disciples. But given the circumstances, a likely interpretation is that Jesus was asking Peter if he loved Jesus more than he loved catching fish. In other words, did he love Jesus more than he loved his profession.

That probing question is another in the set we need to ask ourselves to determine what is keeping us from spiritual renewal. The way we answer "What is it you want?" (Matthew 20:21, NIV) and "Do you love me more than these?"

(John 21:15) will determine whether or not we'll be successful in opening the lock on our desires. And that will determine not only the direction of our lives but also the destiny of our souls.

If your pursuit of earthly things leaves you no time or energy to pursue God, answer the question Jesus asked Peter: "Do you love me more than these?" If you can honestly answer yes, then you are ready to figure out which keys will fit the lock on your soul's desires.

Thoughts: Loving God with My Mind

At age twenty-one, Marcia met a man who swept her off her feet. David was everything she'd ever wanted in a husband and more. Marcia believed she could rely on words from God she perceived through signs and feelings, and after her second meeting with David she was convinced that he was God's chosen man for her.

When Marcia told the women in her prayer group about her new love, they quickly agreed that David was perfect for her and began praying that God would bring the two together.

Whenever Marcia and David talked, he always used flattering and affectionate words. He never said much about himself, but Marcia appreciated that because it proved to her that he wasn't self-centered. He never said much about being with her, either, but there was plenty of opportunity for that later on, Marcia reasoned, believing that she ought to trust God to make things happen in his time.

David lived in another city and called Marcia every couple of weeks, but she longed to talk to him more often. On several occasions, she called her friends and asked them to pray that he would call. Invariably, it seemed, he would call within twenty-four hours.

At one meeting of the prayer group, three women

brought the same verse of Scripture to Marcia: "Whatsoever you ask in prayer believing, you shall receive." Together the group claimed that Scripture for Marcia, telling her that if she would believe God, David would be hers.

Marcia started a journal in which she wrote to God and then wrote what she "heard in her heart" to be his answers to her questions. The answers always confirmed her belief that someday she and David would be together. Her faith in God grew more and more entangled with her desire to be with David, and before long she was convinced that God *had to* bring the two of them together because her dialogue with him had revealed his plans.

The sad end to this story is that David and Marcia never did get together. As it turned out, David was already married. He was simply playing a cruel, flirtatious game with a vulnerable young woman. When Marcia learned the truth from mutual friends, her faith in God disintegrated. She believed God had participated in the deceit by allowing her to believe a lie.

For two years, Marcia refused to pray, go to church, or see her Christian friends, and during that time she had two affairs with non-Christian men. Feeling used and abused, she finally fell on her knees before God in search of answers.

Little by little, Marcia is returning to faith that is founded on truth she did not recognize before: that God is neither obligated to reveal the future to her nor does he have to give her everything she thinks she needs.

Because we worship an unseen God, and because we are emotional and imaginative people, we have a tendency to "create" a God who serves our longings. Our friends, meanwhile, wanting us to be happy, sometimes contribute to our idolatry by participating with us in our mind games and mental image building by neglecting to remind us that God sometimes acts in ways beyond our understanding.

God's will is not hidden in cryptic Bible verses that we can apply to any and all situations. God is not a cosmic bellhop on call to meet our every whim with a supernatural response.

Jesus taught us to pray, "*Your* kingdom come. *Your* will be done," not "*My* kingdom come, *my* will be done." There are times when God may give us a glimpse of what he is going to do in our lives, but he is under no obligation to do so. God tells us to trust him even when we cannot see what he is doing or anticipate what is around the next bend.

Discouragement, disillusionment, doubt, and some forms of depression result from faulty thinking. Discouragement is the inevitable result of believing a lie we tell ourselves. Disillusionment is the result of believing a lie someone else tells us. Doubt results from incomplete or unreliable information. And some forms of depression develop because we feel helpless to find truth.

Marcia ended up with all of the above due to her misinformation about God and her misuse of Scripture. In a way, she was like the people Jesus spoke of in his famous illustration about the difference between wise and foolish people (see Luke 6:46-49).

The wise build on the rock of truth; they hear Jesus' words and obey. But the foolish build on shifting sand; they hear Jesus' words and interpret them to fit their own understanding.

In telling this story, Jesus asked, "Why do you keep calling me 'Lord, Lord!' when you don't do what I say?" (Luke 6:46). In other words, what good is it to have a God who doesn't know as much as you do? If you're so smart, what do you need God for?

When the floods of adversity come, people who live by truth may get wet, but they won't be washed away. People who live by their own understanding, however, will be tossed by doubt and swept away by disillusionment because the god they thought they knew seems to be turning against them.

People like Marcia want a "Lord" who will do as they say, not vice versa. But no such god exists, so that's what they end up with—no god at all.

When we fail to love God with our minds, we make ourselves vulnerable to all kinds of false teaching and we set ourselves up for serious disappointment.

If that describes your situation, ask yourself if you are willing to let go of your false ideas about God and get to know the true and living God. If you can honestly answer yes, determine which keys will unlock the door that is keeping you from loving God with your mind and begin using them.

Habits: Loving God with My Strength

From the time Keith was a teenager, he found ways to get alcohol into his system. He started by having beers with his high school buddies, and in a matter of weeks he was using alcohol on a daily basis. His parents were executives in a family-owned business and were seldom home, so Keith had easy access to their liquor cabinet. Drinking gave him something to look forward to when he came home to an empty house.

Keith became a Christian during college and quickly learned that his church friends weren't as tolerant of alcohol use as were his old friends. Some had an occasional beer or glass of wine, but Keith knew they would disapprove of how much he drank, so he never let them know.

Years passed, and Keith married Jamie. By now Keith was making a good income, and he found a socially acceptable way to make alcohol a regular part of his life. He and Jamie became connoisseurs of fine wine, traveling to wine countries and collecting special vintages. Jamie was able to enjoy the hobby without complications, but she began to wonder about Keith. Did he really delight in the art of wine making or had he simply found a sophisticated way to cover his addiction?

Keith laughed about her concerns. "Have you ever seen me drunk?" he asked.

Jamie had to admit that she hadn't, but something didn't seem quite right. Keith sometimes would forget entire conversations. And he always seemed impatient for four o'clock, the time he allowed himself to begin drinking.

People like Keith are called "functioning alcoholics." They are able to do their jobs, fulfill their obligations, manage their lives, and continue to function while still being hooked on alcohol.

Stopping an addiction is not easy, especially when addictive substances are involved that require physical as well as emotional detoxification. But addictions, compulsions, and obsessions, no matter how "well managed," are not and cannot be part of a healthy spiritual life. No one can experience spiritual renewal while allowing lesser "gods" to rule their lives.

Throughout Scripture, God refuses to tolerate idols or false gods. Obsessive thoughts, compulsive behaviors, and addictive habits are a form of idolatry and must be seen as such, as Dr. David Allen writes:

> Any problem, person, or pleasure occupying your waking or sleeping moments which distracts you from your faith, influences your passions, or pulls you away from your Christian community, has in essence been elevated to godlike status in your life. It has become your God.[1]

Surrender to God always includes this prayer: "Lord, reveal to me anything that is between you and me." When we seek God and surrender to him, it is important that we set no part of our life apart from his authority. This is difficult for addicts because denial is so ingrained into their thinking that they truly believe they're hiding nothing.

When we ask God to reveal whatever is standing in the way of total commitment to him, he will show us the truth. And when he does, we're faced with a difficult decision. Will we agree with him and take responsibility for it or continue to remain its slave?

Admitting addictions and finding the courage to deal with them are difficult even for Christians. Keith, for example, excused himself by saying, "I can stop drinking anytime I want to. There's just no reason to stop."

That kind of comment is common among the addicted. And here are a few more:

"We all have our vices."

"I'm just a little weak in the willpower department."

"I don't need it. I just like it."

"It's no big deal."

"It's just the way I am."

Even those who know they have a problem, and may even hate themselves and the problem behavior, find it next to impossible to speak the whole truth about their addiction. It's very hard to say, "I am addicted. I need to stop, but I can't break the addiction without the help of God and other people."

Jamie finally helped Keith face the fact that he was an alcoholic, but it took a long time for him to see the seriousness of his problem. When he did, he got involved with an alcohol support group at their church. After admitting to the group that he was a functioning alcoholic, Keith made himself accountable to them as he worked toward healing.

Part of taking responsibility for an addiction, a compulsion, or an obsession requires dealing with the underlying causes. We need to look beyond the "acting out" of the addiction and figure out what the behavior is distracting us *from*. Why did the problem develop, and what lack are we using it to compensate for? It's not enough to admit the addiction. We must understand and address the unmet needs and untreated emotional injuries that underlie the addiction. Ask questions like these to determine what they might be:

- What is the source of the emotional emptiness that triggers my addiction?
- What is the pain that feeds my addictive cycle?

Keith didn't have to look far. His parents had been just as addicted as he was, but to work, not alcohol. Obsessed with their money-driven ambitions, they neglected their son's emotional needs. Keith was so emotionally removed from his parents, however, that he could no longer feel the hurt he'd experienced as a child. Left with no feelings of anger or sadness, he sensed no need to forgive them. His emotional numbness was as much a symptom of the damage done to Keith as is volatile, uncontrolled anger in others.

In the years that followed his recovery, Keith completed a writing project based on Jesus' parables about the vine and the branches. Because Keith had spent years learning about wine making, he had tremendous knowledge about tending and pruning grapevines, gathering the fruit, and making wine. He self-published a small book and gave it away as a testimony of his walk with God. His former addiction and success at breaking free provided him with the wisdom and credibility he needed to convey to others God's healing power.

Alcoholism is an obvious addiction, and one that has

been researched, discussed, and treated in dozens of ways. Other addictions or addictive behaviors are not as easily recognized. To determine whether or not you have an addictive, compulsive, or obsessive pattern in your life, answer the following questions as honestly as you can:

- Do I make my plans fit around a particular behavior or person?
- Do I think about it all the time?
- Does it distract me from doing my best work?
- Has it ever created problems with others?
- Has it ever caused me financial problems?
- Could it hurt me physically, emotionally, or spiritually?
- Is it a secret?
- Does it make me feel guilty?
- Do I do it more often than I used to?
- Do I make and break promises to myself about it?
- Does it cause me to compromise my morals or values?

Addictions, obsessions, and compulsions tell us a great deal about ourselves. They show us our fears and point out our inability to live independent of God and others. But they can also remind us that sin, though a part of our human condition, can be defeated. Even though we are unable to overcome our own sin, God is. The power that raised Jesus from the dead is available to us to overcome sin. There is great strength in saying, "I can't. He can. I'll let him."

Jesus displayed his power over sin by exercising his power over physical disease. Among the people Jesus healed were two blind men sitting by the roadside outside Jericho. When they heard that Jesus was coming that way, they began shouting, "Lord, Son of David, have mercy on us!"

The crowd told them to be quiet, but they only shouted louder, "Lord, Son of David, have mercy on us!"

Jesus stopped in the road and called, "What do you want me to do for you?"

"Lord," they said, "we want to see!"

Jesus felt sorry for them and touched their eyes. Instantly they could see! Then they followed him. (See Matthew 20:29-34.)

The question Jesus asked the two blind men will help us determine what locks are keeping us in the bondage of unhealthy habits and preventing us from loving him with all our strength.

Do we want Jesus to give us only temporary relief from our circumstances or do we want permanent relief from our debilitating condition? Many of the blind beggars Jesus encountered probably wanted only a handout to get them through another day.

If we can honestly answer, "Lord, I want my sight," Jesus will enable us to see. But many who say they want to see immediately shut their eyes when they see the frightening truth about themselves.

To witness another powerful example of the two-in-one nature of physical and spiritual healing, we can walk alongside Jesus on his way to Jerusalem for a feast of the Jews. Near the Temple we pass the pool of Bethesda where many blind, lame, and paralyzed people lay waiting to be healed. One man there had been an invalid for thirty-eight years. When Jesus saw him and learned that he had been in this condition for such a long time, he asked him, "Do you want to get well?"

"Sir," the invalid replied, "I have no one to help me into the pool when the water is stirred. While I am trying to get in, someone else goes down ahead of me."

Then Jesus said to him, "Get up! Pick up your mat and walk." At once the man was cured; he picked up his mat and walked. (See John 5:1-9, NIV.)

Considering the man's situation, the question Jesus asked seems almost ridiculous. Of course the man wanted to get well. Why else would he be there? But perhaps the question isn't as ridiculous as it first seems. Many people who've been afflicted with a physical or psychological ailment for a long time become so "attached" to it that they have no identity apart from it. They may say they want to get rid of it, but when they are offered health they find it too frightening to accept. Too many things will change. There is security in affliction, just as there is security in addiction. That is why, for people battling addictions, compulsions, and obsessions, the question Jesus asked the man lying at the pool of Bethesda is amazingly relevant. Spiritual renewal cannot take place until we are able to honestly say we want the strength to walk away from our lame excuses and paralyzing habits. If the lock on your life is an uncontrollable habit, ask yourself the question Jesus asked the man beside the pool of Bethesda: "Do you want to get well?" If you can honestly answer yes, begin using the keys to unlock your strength.

Relationships: Loving My Neighbor As Myself

Ron has had a long-term friendship with Sarah that dates back to college.

After they both married fifteen years ago, they continued their friendship even though both of their spouses have expressed discomfort about it. Ron's wife even accused him of having an emotional affair with Sarah.

Both Ron and Sarah say they have been careful about what they talk about and where they meet for lunch. "There's nothing hidden from our spouses," they both say. "We just go back a long way."

When Ron told his men's accountability group about his

wife's accusation, one of the men spoke up. "Ron, you need to listen to your wife," Dale said. "I believe you when you say there's nothing going on, but if you're letting that friendship upset your wife, maybe you haven't really surrendered it to the Lord."

Ron didn't say much at the time, but he couldn't get Dale's words out of his mind. He began to wonder whether he really had surrendered his friendship with Sarah to the Lord. Over the next few days, Ron realized that Dale had been right. The next week at his small-group meeting he thanked Dale for confronting him. Then he admitted that he'd been holding onto his friendship with Sarah at the expense of his marriage because he was attracted to her.

After seeing the truth and admitting it to those who cared for him, Ron surrendered this part of his life to God, and he took responsibility for setting some new, healthy limits in his friendship with Sarah. Ron's relationship with Sarah was not sinful in the legalistic sense. But it was improper because it was more important to him than his wife's sense of security in their marriage.

Two other types of relationships that reveal our failure to love others as we love ourselves are those that are dependent and those that are estranged. Although they are at opposite ends of the scale of unhealthy relationships, it is not unusual for one person to have both. Those who form overly dependent relationships in one sphere of life— perhaps with their children—often alienate people in another—perhaps those in authority.

Relating is never easy. Two imperfect people form a relationship that can be nothing other than imperfect. But fairy tales and Hollywood would have us believe otherwise. So we keep searching for the perfect friend or mate and keep being disillusioned by imperfection. As a result, we bounce from one imperfect relationship to another, always hoping this will be the one that meets our needs.

People determined to find perfection are destined for disillusionment. And at the end of all our bouncing around, we'll have nothing to show for it except bruised and broken hearts.

But it doesn't have to be that way. The challenge in relationships is to allow weakness and imperfection in others. Though we need to set boundaries to protect ourselves from abuse, we must beware of setting them so close that we keep people out unnecessarily. Healthy boundaries allow for imperfection, irritation, and inferiority. They are the things that polish our rough edges and make us better reflectors of the image of our Creator.

One of our greatest challenges is to look honestly at ourselves and acknowledge what we do to contribute to our own problems. Think about the people around you and consider the following questions. Ask the Holy Spirit to show you where you need to make changes and how you might use the spiritual concepts in this book to do so.

- What percentage of my relationships are warm, peaceful, and supportive?
- How do I account for their success?
- What attempts have I made to make difficult relationships more peaceful?
- Are people afraid to make waves around me? Are they safe with me, or are they "peaceable" because they dare not be otherwise?
- What are the common elements in my struggles with people?
- Do the same patterns keep repeating themselves in my relationships?
- Do I keep running into the same kind of troublesome relationships and wonder why they keep happening?

- Am I attracted to a specific type of person even though that type of person is bad for me?
- Have my out-of-control emotions left emotional or psychological scars on people I love?

If all is well, thank God and submit the future to his ongoing protection, wisdom, and grace. If all is not well, begin examining your relationships—with those you love, those you don't love as much as you should, and those you don't even like. Look for the ways you relate to people that defy or ignore God's social design. Are you stubborn, unkind, selfish, demanding, controlling, manipulative? What other patterns do you see that are ungodly? Look for opportunities to surrender these habits to God's righteous rule.

The quality of our relationships is an indication of our spiritual, emotional, and psychological condition. A healthy relationship with God will transform our relationships with people. The Bible makes this clear with these words:

> If someone says, "I love God," but hates a Christian brother or sister, that person is a liar; for if we don't love people we can see, how can we love God, whom we cannot see? And he has given us this command: Those who love God must also love their Christian brothers and sisters.   1 John 4:20-21

The Christians in Corinth took great pride in their spirituality, but they were treating each other terribly. Their relationships were a mess. Some were involved in sinful sexual relationships; one man went so far as to have an affair with his stepmother. Others were just plain rude. When Paul tried to correct them, he made it clear that their self-perceived spiritual attainments meant nothing if their relationships with others were not characterized by godly love. He wrote this well-loved passage that is often read at weddings but too seldom applied to nonromantic relationships:

> If I could speak all the languages of earth and of angels, but didn't love others, I would only be a noisy gong or a clanging cymbal. If I had the gift of prophecy, and if I understood all of God's secret plans and possessed all knowledge, and if I had such faith that I could move mountains, but didn't love others, I would be nothing. If I gave everything I have to the poor and even sacrificed my body, I could boast about it; but if I didn't love others, I would have gained nothing.
>
> Love is patient and kind. Love is not jealous or boastful or proud or rude. It does not demand its own way. It is not irritable, and it keeps no record of being wronged. It does not rejoice about injustice but rejoices whenever the truth wins out. Love never gives up, never loses faith, is always hopeful, and endures through every circumstance. 1 Corinthians 13:1-7

Since love is the proof of true spirituality, every person pursuing spiritual renewal has to deal with the challenge of relationships.

As we use the spiritual concepts presented here to relate to people in a godly way, God will give us the grace to be at peace with others and to become a peacemaker. In becoming a peacemaker, we begin working with God to reconcile to him a world that is separated by sin and rebellion. And in so doing we become heirs to this promise: "God blesses those who work for peace, for they will be called the children of God" (Matthew 5:9).

A popular wrist strap worn by believers bears the letters WWJD, which represent the question "What Would Jesus Do?" This slogan is our generation's version of *In His Steps,* a best-selling book by Charles Sheldon that used the form of a novel to explore the same question one hundred years ago.

No faith but Christianity can ask such a question of their deity because no other deity has dared to live a mortal life. No other god has come to this planet blighted by sin and evil to show the way to overcome it. None but the true God would dare to do so. Evil will not tolerate goodness, so only a God who is more powerful than all evil could risk coming here. This truth, which we call the doctrine of the incarnation, is one of the most amazing tenets of Christianity. Imagine. The God we believe in became human just like us.

- He didn't remain aloof and bellow instructions from above.
- He didn't just visit earth to have a little fun with weak mortals—as did the mythological Greek gods and goddesses.
- He didn't stay in a tomb, embalmed like an Egyptian mummy.
- He didn't set up a throne and demand worship.
- He didn't set up a kingdom and demand service.

Our God came and lived among us so we could behold his glory.

> So the Word became human and made his home among us. He was full of unfailing love and faithfulness. And we have seen his glory, the glory of the Father's one and only Son.
>
> John 1:14

Dave and I can explain the principles we've outlined in this book and tell you how to live by them. And of course we do our best to live by them ourselves. But we don't always succeed. Evidence of our failure is all around us. But Jesus didn't just tell us how to live; he came and showed us how. He doesn't ask us to do anything he hasn't done himself. In fact, the biblical account of Christ's life provides evidence that Jesus himself practiced the principles we've outlined.

Jesus surrendered himself to God

Jesus pleaded with God to spare him from the agony of crucifixion, but when God said that wasn't an option, he willingly submitted. "Father, if you are willing, please take this cup of suffering away from me. Yet I want your will to be done, not mine" (Luke 22:42). "[Jesus] humbled himself and became obedient to death—even death on a cross!" (Philippians 2:8, NIV).

Jesus saw the truth

In an unprecedented remark, Jesus went beyond claiming to see truth; he proclaimed that he was the embodiment of truth: "I am the way, the truth, and the life. No one can come to the Father except through me. If you had really known me, you would know who my Father is. From now on, you do know him and have seen him!" (John 14:6-7).

Jesus spoke the truth

The book of Matthew records thirty times that Jesus said, "I tell you the truth" (NIV). He once proclaimed that his purpose in coming to earth was to testify to the truth: "I was born and came into the world to testify to the truth. All who love the truth recognize that what I say is true" (John 18:37).

Jesus took responsibility for tasks assigned to him

Imagine never being distracted by your own desires, never getting sidetracked by other people's expectations, never trying to accomplish your own agenda. That's how Jesus lived.

"I have come down from heaven to do the will of God who sent me, not to do my own will" (John 6:38).

Jesus forgave

Hanging from a Roman cross, dying for crimes he did not commit, the innocent Son of God uttered words of forgiveness few of us can even imagine: "Father, forgive them, for they don't know what they are doing" (Luke 23:34).

Jesus was transformed

Even though Jesus was the perfect Son of God, he changed during the course of his lifetime. "Jesus grew in wisdom and in stature and in favor with God and all the people" (Luke 2:52).

Jesus persevered to the end

Although God failed to answer his prayer for deliverance the way he wanted, Jesus didn't become stubborn and refuse to cooperate with God's plan for the justification and reconciliation of the world. He accomplished his first assignment: "This is the will of God, that I should not lose even one of all those he has given me, but that I should raise them up at the last day" (John 6:39) and "I did not lose a single one of those you have given me" (John 18:9). And he is still at work: "I am with you always, even to the end of the age" (Matthew 28:20).

As you begin following the example of Jesus and using these spiritual concepts, keep in mind the Scripture passages at the beginning of this chapter:

> I want them to be encouraged and knit together by strong ties of love. I want them to have complete confidence that they understand God's mysterious plan, which is Christ himself. In him lie hidden all the treasures of wisdom and knowledge. Colossians 2:2-3

> Though the LORD is very great and lives in heaven, he will make Jerusalem his home of justice and righteousness. In that day he will be your sure foundation, providing a rich store of salvation, wisdom, and knowledge. The fear of the LORD will be your treasure.
>
> Isaiah 33:5-6

If confusion seems to be the reigning force in your life, remember the last phrase of both verses: "In [Christ] lie hidden all the treasures of wisdom and knowledge" and "the fear of the LORD will be your treasure."

Notes

1. David Allen, *Shattering the Gods Within* (Chicago: Moody, 1994).